USS Arizona *in mid-career, as modernized 1929–1931.*

USS ARIZONA (BB 39)

by Norman Friedman, Arthur D. Baker, III, Arnold S. Lott, LCDR, USN (Ret.), and Robert F. Sumrall, HTC, USNR

THE USS *Arizona* (BB39) was the third ship of the U. S. Navy to bear that name. She was named for the state of Arizona, the 48th state to join the union; the first and second *Arizona*s were named for the Territory of Arizona. Although *Arizona* was destroyed during the Japanese attack on Pearl Harbor, 7 December 1941—with the greatest loss of life ever incurred in any one disaster in U.S. naval history—the U. S. flag still flies over the wreck of the ship in Pearl Harbor. Many other ships lost during World War II were honored by having their names given almost immediately to newer ships, but there will probably never be another *Arizona* in the U. S. Navy; that name will belong forever to the ship and her crew that lies at the bottom of Pearl Harbor.

The first *Arizona* was an 1859-vintage iron-hulled sidewheel steamer. She was originally a Confederate blockade runner named *Carolina,* and was captured by Union forces on 28 October 1862. After beig renamed,

she was commissioned in the Navy on 9 March 1863 and operated on the Gulf of Mexico and on the rivers of Texas and Louisiana, as a unit of the West Coast Blockading Squadron. She displaced 959 tons, was 200 feet long, carried four 32-pounder smoothbore cannon, one 30-pounder rifled cannon, and one 12-pounder rifled cannon. She had a crew of 91 officers and men.

Arizona took part in the capture of Aurelia, Louisiana, on 23 March 1863, the destruction of the Confederate ship *Queen of the West* on 14 April 1863, and the capture of Butte a la Rose on 20 April 1863. She fought Confederate ships on the Red River early in May of 1863, and joined in the attacks of Fort Beauregard, Louisiana on 7 May and Fort De Russy, Louisiana two days later. Her final action during the year was during the attack on Sabine Pass, Texas, on 7–8 September. From then until November 1864, she operated on the blockade of the Texas

1

USS Arizona, *as modernized, heading into a sea leading another modernized battleship, the USS* Nevada. *The clock of the foremast is a "concentration dial" by means of which transmitted her firing range to the ship ahead of her.*

coast; she was then assigned flagship duty on the Mississippi River. On 27 February 1865, she caught fire and was destroyed at a point 38 miles below New Orleans.

The second *Arizona* carried the name for less than three months during 1869, and was never in active service. She was a screw frigate, built at the Philadelphia Navy Yard where she was launched as the *Neshaminy* on 5 October 1865. The wooden-hulled ship, displacing 3,850 tons, was towed to the New York Navy Yard for installation of her engines, but the work was not completed and she was laid up in 1869. Her name was changed to *Arizona* on 15 May 1869, and changed again to *Nevada* on 12 August of that year. Examination showed her to be in such poor condition that she was not worth completing, and the hulk was sold for scrap in 1874.

Design Background

Every warship is designed to perform a specific mission. *Arizona*'s mission was to fight as a unit of the battle line in a main fleet battle against Japan for the control of the Pacific Ocean. Every element of her design was in consideration of conditions her designers expected her to encounter in such a battle. When the ship was designed in 1912, the accepted concept of a great naval battle was that of two lines of battleships steaming on roughly parallel courses (pretty much as ships did in Nelson's time) while shelling each other in hope of inflicting decisive damage. Meanwhile, destroyers would dart out from behind the battle line in an attempt to fire torpedoes at the huge targets in the enemy line. In those days, battleships too could fire torpedoes at each other.

The significance of the Pacific as a battle ground was twofold. In contrast to conditions in the North Sea, which preoccupied British and German strategic thought, Pacific weather is quite often very clear, so that—in theory—gunnery could be effective at extreme ranges. The fleet with guns able to fire at the longest range could always get in the first shots. *Arizona*'s armament and armor protection were expressions of the requirements of very long range duelling. Another most important point was the immense size of the Pacific—great distances between possible combat areas and home bases meant that ships had to carry unusually heavy loads of fuel. It also meant that they had to be tough enough to withstand heavy damage—a ship injured in battle might have to steam

2

Modernization included an increase in elevation of the main battery from 15 to 30 degrees, for firing at increased range. Note the .50 cal. machine guns mounted on both masts and the after "concentration dial" just below the fire control top.

thousands of miles to reach a base. For such reasons, *Arizona* was far larger than her European contemporaries. Normal cruising distances for *Arizona* were expected to be about 4,000 miles; European battleships designed primarily for operations in the North Sea might operate over distances of only 400 miles.

World War I operations added a new element to battle at sea—airpower. Aircraft, or more precisely, lighter-than-air Zeppelins were the most effective reconnaissance arm of the German Navy, and the British had to place fighter aircraft on their ships in an effort to drive off the German scouts. The U. S. Navy soon adopted the idea; battleships first had special "flying off" platforms atop their turrets, and later these were replaced by catapults. *Arizona* still had catapults in 1941. Aircraft could also make torpedo attacks previously carried out by destroyers, and they could also drop bombs. Both dangers were recognized quite early; in the 20s and 30s American battleships such as *Arizona* had some of the heaviest antiaircraft armaments in the world—although World War II combat proved that they needed still heavier AA armament. One of the purposes in the extensive reconstruction carried out on *Arizona* in 1928–31 was toward further protection against air attack; extra deck armor was installed and a more effective AA battery was mounted

As a last consideration, aircraft could extend the range of accurate shellfire beyond a ship's horizon by observing the fall of shot around a target and transmitting the results to the firing ship. As the U.S. Navy had enthusiastically adopted a policy of long-range gun firing, this was an important function; it was made evident by the installation of large

aircraft catapults on all battleships, even though catapults at times interfered with fire of the main battery guns.

When the war in the Pacific began, the rapid growth of airpower meant that battleships would never meet in a surface slug-fest such as the British and German fleets did in the World War I Battle of Jutland. Aircraft carriers became the queens of the fleet, and the traditional striking force of battleships gave way to the fast carrier task force. The old battleships were mostly put out of action at Pearl Harbor on 7 December 1941; those that returned to duty with the fleet were too slow to accompany the fast carriers. To many people, the spectacular destruction of *Arizona* marked the end of the battle line concept. After enormous sums had been spent on her construction, reconstruction, and upkeep for more than twenty years, she had been destroyed by a few aircraft without ever having fired a shot in battle from her main battery.

Yet the old battleships did, in a way, perform their primary mission. The Japanese had to attack the U.S. battle fleet because of the threat it posed to Japanese expansion in Southeast Asia. For twenty years the U.S. had kept it battleships in the Pacific as a warning that it was determined to protect American interests in that vast area. The Japanese took that warning seriously. When they decided to seize the resources of Southeast Asia by force, they regarded the U. S. battle fleet as an obstacle, a deterrent which had to be destroyed if their plans were to be carried out. Their first—and highly successful—move was to hit Pearl Harbor and prevent *Arizona* and the other U. S. battleships there from steaming west to battle.

Pennsylvania *Class*

Between 1910 and 1945, U. S. warships were designed to Characteristics prepared by a senior navy council known as the General Board. *Arizona* was actually the product of the first set of battleship Characteristics, prepared early in 1910. These called for "all or nothing" armor (*see* ARMOR), a main battery of twelve 14-inch guns in triple turrets, an engineering plant operating on oil, and a speed of 21 knots. The 1910 Characteristics were matched to an inadequate Congressional appropriation for the Fiscal Year 1912 program; consequently the two 1912 ships, *Nevada* and *Oklahoma*, were built with two less guns than planned and their speed was reduced by half a knot. Their sketch designs were completed in the spring of 1911.

In June of 1911 the General Board revived its original Characteristics, and the constructors submitted sketch designs early in March of 1912. These allowed for variations in speed and hull form. On 3 April 1912 the General Board selected a design that was considered so satisfactory no further preliminary designs would be required. At that time the Board thought that Congress would provide for four battleships in Fiscal Year 1913—this would allow building battleship numbers 38 through 41. In fact, only one ship, *Pennsylvania* was authorized. The cut in building was in part a congressional reaction to the increase in displacement (and cost) between *Nevada* at 27,500 tons and *Pennsylvania* at 31,400 tons.

	BB 38 & 39	BB 36 & 37	Change
Displacement, full load	32,500	28,400	+ 4,100 tons
Displacement, normal	31,400	27,500	+ 3,900 tons
Length, overall	608'	583'	+ 25 feet
Length, pp	600'	575'	+ 25 feet
Beam, load WL	97'	95'-2''	+ 1'-10''
Draft, mean	28'-10''	28'-6''	+ 4 inches
Draft, max.	29'-10''	29'-7''	+ 3 inches
Main Battery	12-14''	10-14''	+ 2 guns
Speed	21.0 knots	20.53 knots	+ .47 knots

In Fiscal Year 1914 Congress once more authorized only a single battleship, which was to become *Arizona*. There were only minor improvements over *Pennsylvania*, chief among them being the use of flat, rather than curved, armor over the stack uptake area. The time saved by using the plans of *Pennsylvania* allowed builders to start work on the new ship rather quickly, and she was completed only four months after *Pennsylvania*.

The Act of 4 March 1913 specified that the *Arizona* was to be built in a government yard. Once the ship had been authorized, the Bureau of Construction and Repair negotiated with the building yard and a starting date of 15 September 1913 was arranged. If the ship had been built in a commercial yard, bids wold have been required, a process extending over two or three months.

Construction

The first material was ordered on 18 September 1913 and deliveries to the Brooklyn Navy Yard began on 3 November. Preliminary assembly went on in shops within the yard; nothing was erected on the building ways until the keel was laid on 16 March 1914. Meanwhile, the hull was laid out full scale on templates in the "mold loft," so that plates could be cut to size. The keel-laying ceremony marked the start of actual construction.

The frames, or ribs, began to go up the day after the keel was laid. There were 150 frames, spaced at 4-foot intervals. By 2 April enough structural work had been done to allow fitting the first of the athwartships bulkheads which divided the ship into watertight compartments. On 6 July the first large casting was erected. Many such castings were required, including the sternpost which supported the massive rudder. Also, in July the last of the hull plates had been cut to size.

Some 6,000 tons of armor plate had been ordered for the ship, and the first completed plates were delivered to the ways on 20 July: installation of armor plating did not commence until 30 September. In the meantime, construction had progressed to the point where air-testing of compartments, to make sure there were no leaks in watertight bulkheads or decks, began on 24 September. The main belt armor was not installed until after the ship was in the water, so as to keep a minimum of weight on the building ways and slipway.

On 20 May 1915 the rudder was installed, and on 19 June, less than two years after she had been ordered, *Arizona* was launched. She was officially christened by Miss Esther Ross, the daughter of a pioneer citizen of Prescott, Arizona. The turrets were assembled on board after the ship was in the water, with the first one completed on 27 October 1915. The installation of 5-inch guns began on 15 March 1916 and the first heavy 14-inch guns were installed on 7 April. Meanwhile, the belt armor was being fitted, and the superstructure was completed by the end of September.

The precommissioning test commenced with an "inclining experiment." This involved placing heavy weights on deck at one side of the ship to cause a list; the relation between the degree of list and the weight applied was a measure of her stability. She was then taken to sea for trials of her engineering plant.

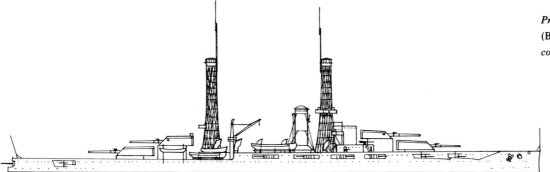

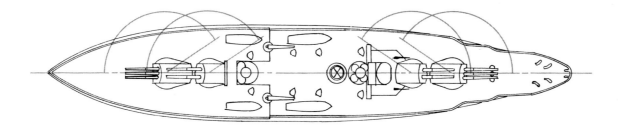

Profile and plan of Nevada (BB 36) *and* Oklahoma (BB 37) *showing arrangement of armament and concentration of fire.*

SCALE 1/1200

0   50   100   200

Profile and plan of Pennsylvania (BB 38) *and* Arizona (BB 39) *showing arrangement of armament and concentration of fire.*

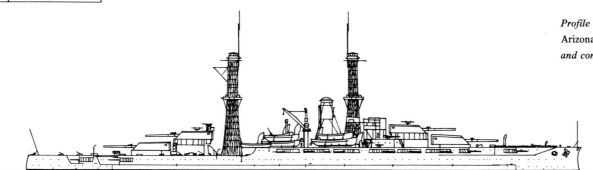

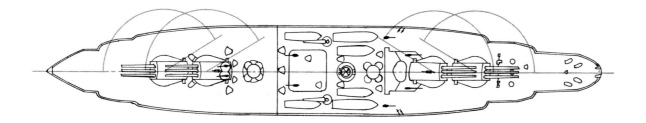

Some hull material (part of the bottom plating) was assembled by the shipway even before the keel was laid. Note the scaffolding erected alongside the shipway to suit the shape of the intended hull.

Amid much ceremony, the keel was laid for USS Arizona *(BB39) on 16 March 1914 and construction was officially underway.*

Compartmentation and Arrangement

The hull was transversely framed of riveted steel construction. There were three decks extending the full length of the ship: the main deck, second deck, and third deck. All three decks were a constant height above the keel with no sheer.

There were two platform decks below the third deck, extending forward from and aft of the machinery spaces. A double bottom was fitted for the entire length between the peak tanks. Transversely the tanks followed the shape of the hull up to the sloping splinter deck forming a solid shelf on which the side armor was mounted. (*See* MIDSHIP *and* TYPE *sections.*)

The midship section shape was full. The ends were fine with a protruding bulbous bow which considerably reduced the wave making resistance at higher speeds, and a cruiser stern with one large semi-balanced rudder. The deadwood was cut away for a short distance forward of the rudder and each shaft was supported by a single strut just forward of the propeller hub. Side docking keels were fitted in way of the torpedo bulkheads in addition to the usual bilge keels.

The forecastle deck extended forward from the "break" of the deck at frame 88 and just forward of the mainmast. The main deck was thus sheltered forward from breaking seas and could be used for crew accommodations and machinery rooms for the windlass gear as well as the 5-inch casemates. The forecastle deck was, in effect, a superstructure deck. That portion of the main deck aft of frame 88 was open to the weather and referred to as the "quarterdeck" area.

The second deck was used primarily for accommodations. The area forward of No. 1 barbette was occupied by the CPOs and sick bay, the shipfitters' and carpenters' shops, and laundry were located around No. 1 and No. 2 barbettes; crew berthing and divisional offices were amidships and outboard of the boiler uptakes and air intake spaces, and officers' country was aft of frame 91.

The third deck was mostly allocated to storerooms. Boiler uptakes penetrated the deck individually and were trunked into a common casing amidships. Longitudinal ammunition passages were outboard of the uptakes and extending between No. 1 and No. 2 barbettes. Mess attendants were berthed around the aft end of No. 3 barbette and the area aft of frame 127 was officers' country. The splinter deck, which sloped down and outboard from below the third deck, was kept void.

The hull housed the machinery spaces amidships below the third deck. The first and second platform decks were not continuous and extended forward and aft from the boundaries of the machinery spaces.

The hold was the lowest deck; extending from the stem to the rudder post it carried the foundations for the main machinery. Reserve feed water tanks were built above the hold in the boiler rooms giving the

These four views show various stages of the construction progress. From left to right, above and below, these shots were taken 2 April, 3 May, 2 June, and 2 July 1914. The first photo shows raised floors erected to support the machinery; they would form additional tankage underneath. The second shows much of the holding bulkhead, the inner side of the torpedo protection system. The frame tops are angled to support the sloping side of the protective deck. By the date of the fourth photograph the bulkheads for the machinery spaces have been erected.

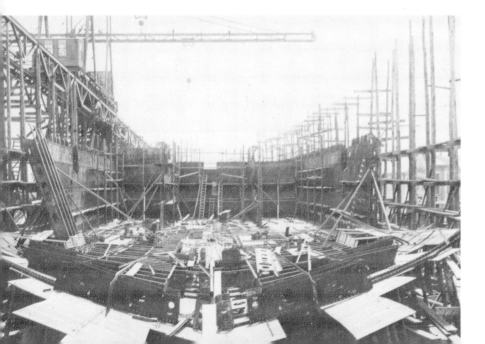

Arizona nearly ready for launching, 18 June 1915, with much of her underwater hull visible. One of her torpedo tubes is visible just above the outboard propeller shaft. A pair of similar tubes forward was deleted during construction. Also visible are the unusual bilge keels which

effect of a triple bottom in that area. The double bottom tanks, between the hold and the shell of the ship, were used to store additional feed water, potable water, oil. Many were kept void.

Superstructure

The superstructure consisted of two deckhouses on the forecastle deck. Compared with earlier designs, *Arizona*'s superstructure seemed austere.

The forward deckhouse was built around the aft end of No. 2 barbette enclosing the armored communications tube between the conning tower and "central." The captain's stateroom was located in the starboard side of the deckhouse and the ship's bakery occupied the port side.

The after deckhouse was located aft of the stack and just forward of the break. It contained the crew's galley, butcher shop, and stowage for perishables.

consisted of two separate sections; what appears to be another keel below the after bilge keel is a docking keel, to help support the ship in drydock. All ten 5-inch casemates are clearly visible.

Bridge and Conning Tower

A small open bridge was fitted to the sides and aft of the conning tower and high enough to see over the conning tower for maneuvering the ship. Directly below the bridge was the chart house platform with open wings and an enclosure for the chart table between them. The entire structure was supported from the superstructure deckhouse forward.

An armored conning tower was fitted aft of No. 2 turret and high enough to give an unobstructed view of the stem through the viewing ports, and over the roofs of the forward turrets. The sides were 16 inches thick with three viewing ports across the front and three on each side. The ship control area occupied the forward end and fire control took up the rear portion of the small elliptical space. The massive weight of the structure was supported and kept rigidly in place by a nest of

9

Launching of the USS Arizona *at the Brooklyn Navy Yard, 19 June 1915. Miss Esther Ross, from Prescott, Arizona, the daughter of Mr. W. W. Ross, a prominent pioneer of Arizona, sponsored the ship. Miss Ross christened the ship with two bottles, one containing American Champagne and the other with water from the Roosevelt Dam on the Arizona River.*

three longitudinal and three transverse bulkheads which extended down to the armored deck providing a firm foundation. The armored conning tower tube, which had an inside diameter of five feet, extended down to the overhead of "central" on the third deck.

Masts

Two tall cage masts of equal height were fitted to carry a spotting position atop each. The cages also carried the usual array of yardarms, antenna supports, searchlight platforms, torpedo control platforms, and tall topmasts, which could be lowered vertically for passage under low obstructions such as the Brooklyn Bridge.

The structure was formed of an open weave of two inclined sets of tubing forming sets of triangles which gave rigidity to the whole asembly. At the intersections of the inclined members, tubes formed horizontal circumferential rings, and wire gratings were fitted at several levels within the mast providing landings for the inclined ladders that gave access to the searchlight platforms and spotting tops. The diameter increased toward the base giving stability to the structure, which was clamped together at all tube intersections.

More tubes were provided than were actually needed, therefore, the loss or damage of several members would not affect the strength or rigidity of the mast. The individual members of the structure were light enough so they were not likely to initiate fuze action if struck and the masts were not considered shell traps.

In operations with the British Grand Fleet during World War I, the cage masts did not appear to be nearly as sturdy as the tripod masts used by the Royal Navy. Many U.S. Naval officers became convinced that cage masts were an unnecessary complication. During her reconstruction *Arizona*'s cage masts were replaced with tripods.

Searchlights

Eight searchlights were fitted. Four were mounted on a platform on the foremast well above the bridge, and four were mounted on a platform on the mainmast well above the 3-inch antiaircraft guns fitted atop No. 3 turret. The lights were manually controlled by operators stationed at the lights.

Armament

The main battery of guns of a battleship were the whole reason for her existence: these massive weapons hurled salvos of heavy projectiles at targets well beyond the visual horizon. The secondary battery consisted of smaller caliber weapons intended primarily for defense against light surface vessels. Battleships of the late 19th century and early 20th century often carried several different sizes of guns. The British revolutionized battleship design in 1906 by building the "all big gun" HMS *Dreadnought* with ten heavy caliber guns, and a uniform secondary armament of light guns for anti-torpedo boat defense. The navies of the world then began a race to develop larger more powerful "Dreadnought" type battleships, and guns quickly increased in size, from the 12-inch weapons of HMS *Dreadnought* to 13.5-inch, 14-inch, 15-inch, 16-inch, and in a few cases, 18-inch weapons. The 14-inch/45 caliber guns mounted in *Arizona* and *Pennsylvania* were the third installation of that size in the U. S. Navy; they were first used in *Texas* and *New York* as replies to the 13.5-inch weapons of the British *Orion* class.

Main Battery

Arizona was designed to mount twelve 14-inch guns in four triple turrets, two forward and two aft. The guns could fire a 1400 pound armor piercing (AP) shell to a range of 18,000 yards, which in 1914 was considered the practical limit for successful gunnery. World War One battle experience suggested otherwise, and much work was done between the wars to extend the range. (*See* ARMAMENT *section following* RECONSTRUCTION *for details.*)

The turrets were elaborate structures extending deep into the ship. At the top was an armored gunhouse, into the front of which was fitted the massive triple slide in which the guns recoiled. This mounting was first introduced in the *Nevada* class and criticized on the theory that a single hit could disable the three guns at once. Ships subsequent to *Arizona* had individual slides for each gun, but provisions were made for locking all of the guns in a turret together. The triple slide was elevated by electrical power turning long screws which fitted into the slide near the breechblocks.

The gunhouse, the visible part of the structure, rotated on a roller bearing race within the fixed armored tube or barbette. The barbettes protected the shells, powder hoists, and gun training and elevating machinery. From the gunhouse hung rotating levels containing the hoists, and their electric motors, as well as 41 projectiles. Another 291 projectiles could be stowed in fixed magazines. Approximately 100 rounds per gun were normally carried. Special efforts were made throughout the structure to prevent flashback moving down from the turret into the shell and powder storage area. The British had had several casualties of this nature at Jutland.

Secondary Battery

Arizona's secondary battery consisted of twenty-two high velocity 5-inch/51 caliber guns for defense against torpedo attack from destroyers. They were mounted in armored casemates and distributed around the ship so as to cover every angle of approach. They were fitted in the casemates so as to allow an arc of fire of between 90 degrees and 120 degrees.

Two of the guns were fitted atop the deckhouse on the forecastle deck abreast the conning tower, eight were mounted on each side of the main deck under the shelter of the forecastle deck, and two were installed on each side of the second deck aft near the stern. In actual operations, all of the guns proved to be wet, even in moderate weather. The forecastle itself was a reaction to charges of wetness in previous designs; it afforded shelter to the gun positions by preventing the sea from coming in—all at one time—but the casemate closures could never be made satisfactorily tight and decks in the wardroom area and officers' country were commonly awash. In later designs, attempts were made to keep the secondary battery dry by placing the guns on the superstructure deckhouse atop the forecastle. This feature was extended to *Arizona* as part of her reconstruction. (*See* ARMAMENT *section following* RECONSTRUCTION *for details.*)

The 5-inch/51 caliber guns were unsuitable for use against aircraft. The long barrel, which gave the gun its high velocity and flat trajectory, was easily pointed against surface targets. However, these characteristics made it difficult to maneuver the gun fast enough to track aircraft. In addition, an antiaircraft version would have required a high mounting which would have made fast loading difficult. These drawbacks meant that special antiaircraft weapons were required.

Antiaircraft Battery, 3-Inch/50 Caliber

The U. S. Navy adopted the 3-inch/50 caliber semi-automatic gun as the standard weapon for the antiaircraft batteries of battleships and battle cruisers. Its characteristics offered the best balance of the requirements for rapid pointing and training, rapid loading and firing, high muzzle velocity, and large enough caliber to produce a good-sized shrapnel or high-explosive burst in the air.

Arizona leaving the Brooklyn Navy Yard for her shakedown cruise. As originally outfitted she had very little superstructure and only a small bridge area. Rangefinders are visible atop both masts; her topmasts, which support the radio antennas, have been stepped down for passage under the bridges across the East River.

In March 1917 *Arizona* received four 3-inch/50 caliber mounts; two were fitted to the top of turret No. 3 and two were installed atop the superstructure deck house on the forecastle deck just forward of the break.

Battery Barrage

All of these guns fired relatively slowly; they were expected to put up a barrage of exploding shells at a distance from the ship. It was hoped that this barrage would deter level bombers. Against torpedo planes coming in at low level, the anti-destroyer guns could be fired into the sea, creating splashes through which the aircraft (in theory) could not fly. The plan was never tried, although the big guns of German warships may have so splashed a few British aircraft in World War II.

Arizona, 11 May 1918, in American waters. Her topmasts carry radio antennas, visible only through their spreader bars. The two forward and four aft 5-inch casemate mounts have been removed, for mounting aboard merchant ships and auxiliaries. (Also see photo at right)

At anchor in Lynn Haven Roads, May 1918, showing the light colored canvas wind shields on both masts to protect personnel operating the searchlights and stations used to control secondary battery fire against destroyers. Note the four 3-inch antiaircraft guns that have been added; two on the deckhouse abaft the boat cranes and two atop No. 3 turret. The long base rangefinders have been removed from the mastheads.

Torpedo Tubes

The main battery was augmented by two underwater torpedo tubes. A considerable effort was expended on long range torpedoes in many navies prior to World War I, and ranges as great as 15,000 yards were attained. This meant that battleships in the battle line could hit their opponents with torpedoes as well as shells at the ranges envisaged about 1914. Although torpedoes were not likely to make hits because of the lengthy interval between launch and arrival at the target, the consequences of a hit were most impressive. It was argued that a battle line presented so large a target that some hits were inevitable, furthermore, an enemy observer could not see torpedoes being fired from underwater tubes, and "tracks" would theoretically be invisible amid the shell splashes of battle.

The development of longer range gunnery changed matters. Once ships could engage beyond torpedo range, the disadvantages of torpedoes—principally, the large underwater compartments required constituted a weak area in the side protection system—eventually caused their removal.

Both *Arizona* and *Pennsylvania* had been designed for four tubes; two torpedo rooms, one forward and one aft, could each discharge a torpedo to port and starboard. Both ships lost one torpedo room, *Arizona* before her completion.

Fire Control

All guns would be useless without some method of controlling the accuracy of their fire. Prior to 1900, naval engagements were intended to be fought at almost point blank range, and the guns were aimed and fired from the turrets without the aid of optical devices more accurate than a hand held telescope. At that time, in England, Admiral Sir Percy Scott, and later in the United States, Admiral William S. Sims, fought for the introduction of fire control systems whereby the guns were all aimed and fired from one or more central locations. The introduction of the coincidence, and the stereoscopic rangefinder, followed by simple analog computers to predict the variables of target location such as windage and range, increased accurate gunfire from about 4,000 yards in 1900 to well over 20,000 yards only a decade later.

A great premium was placed on the extension of effective range—the range at which hits could be secured—as opposed to the farthest distance that a gun could lob a shell. The gunnery fire control system was designed to feed information to the guns so that the elevation and bearing could be set to hit a rapidly moving target, with coordinates based on where the enemy could be expected to be at the far end of a shell's trajectory as much as half a minute after firing. The main component was the "present range," as estimated by a series of rangefinders: one in each turret and one atop each superfiring turret. Data from the rangefinders was fed into the computers in "central" which was located deep within the ship on the second platform deck where it was protected by the armored citadel. The "present range" was corrected to the required figure by predicting the enemy's position using his, and *Arizona*'s estimated course and speed. Against the figure the performance of the guns had to be considered: this varied according to barrel wear, weather, powder temperature, and latitude—which determined the magnitude of the Coriolus Effect.*

Coriolus Effect—the effect of the rotation of the earth on any object on motion in the air above it. A projectile is deflected to the right in the northern hemisphere, and to the left in the southern hemisphere, with deflection increasing in higher latitudes. (Named for Gaspard Coriolus, a French civil engineer who discovered it.)

USS Pennsylvania *firing a broadside in 1921; she and* Arizona *had near identical appearances at the time. The two aids to concentration firing that were adopted from British experience during World War I are clearly visible: the concentration dial on the mast and the angle deflection markings on the turret side, indicating range and bearing. The platforms halfway up the mast are for secondary battery fire control. They were also used to control the search-lights above, in night action against attacking destroyers.*

All of this data was (literally) cranked into a mechanical computer, and the proper gun elevation and bearing was read off and transmitted to the turrets. When all guns were loaded and aimed, the gunnery officer would fire them together in a single salvo. Falling up to thirty seconds later, the shells would cause large visible splashes in a pattern near the target. This "fall of shot" would be observed by spotting parties on platforms high atop the masts. The first pattern would usually miss and the spotters would feed corrections into "central."

Spotting was crucial to the operation of the system. In theory the computer in "central" could give exact ranges and bearings but the data fed into it had to be exact—enemy ships, for example, would not be signalling their exact speed and course changes. Special efforts were made to protect the spotters in battle. The cage masts which carried the spotting positions were so designed that they could absorb a considerable amount of damage without being brought down, and two positions were provided (two masts) so that in the event one was brought down or disabled, one would survive.

During World War I the Royal Navy devised a means of augmenting existing fire control techniques by passing the enemy's range and bearing from ship to ship along the battle line. Range clocks (Concentration dials) were mounted on both of the cage masts so they could be seen fore and aft. These dials enabled the next ship, ahead and astern, to determine the range at which *Arizona* was firing if they could not spot the target. Bearing scales were painted on the sides of turrets 2 and 3 to allow the next ship in line to determine the bearing of gun fire. At Jutland, one ship could shoot down a lane of clear vision while adjacent ships could not find the target. These simple devices allowed a concentration of fire, enabling a ship to shoot at a target it could not see.

Armor and Protection

The designers of the ship considered shells and torpedoes to be the principal weapons she would encounter. Since she was expected to fight only at long range, it was assumed that only very heavy armor-piercing (AP) shells would strike her. This allowed the designers a considerable economy in armor weight. The reason was that an AP shell exploded only *after* it had passed through thick armor. Conversely, very few AP shells would explode if all they penetrated was ordinary steel plate. Hence, ironically, a man behind either very thin *or* very thick steel would be likely to survive hits by AP shells; but any armor thicknesses between these extremes would only serve to detonate the shell. The resulting rain of steel splinters would do the work of destruction.

Only the U. S. Navy seemed to have completely understood this point. While European battleships retained medium thickness armor, proof only against medium artillery—that is, guns which could not hit at long battle ranges—the U.S. proclaimed the policy of "all or nothing" in armor. "All" meant 13.5-inch armor used extensively along the waterline of a ship; "nothing" meant no armor at all over the secondary

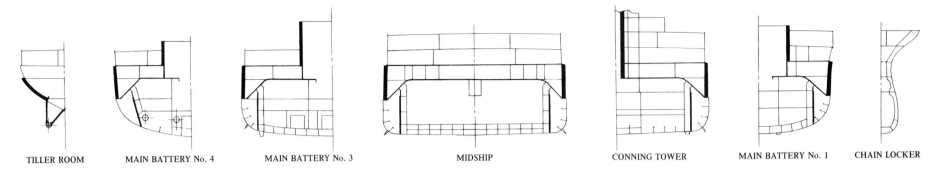

| TILLER ROOM | MAIN BATTERY No. 4 | MAIN BATTERY No. 3 | MIDSHIP | CONNING TOWER | MAIN BATTERY No. 1 | CHAIN LOCKER |

The midship and type sections of the BB 38 and BB 39 class battleships as originally constructed. For details of armor, see GENERAL DATA.

battery. The weight saved by not installing medium weight armor was used to extend the armor belt over a larger area, and to provide protection for the boiler uptakes so that flue gasses would not fill the interior of a ship in battle.

The side armor was intended to resist shells fired almost horizontally. But the navy, which wanted to fight at long ranges, had to face the fact that at those ranges shells would "plunge" at a steep angle and fall upon the deck of a ship rather than hit its side armor. Weight precluded applying enough armor to the deck covering the armor belt to stop big AP shells. But even there it was possible to take advantage of the fuzing characteristics of AP shells in defending against them. In that situation the designers wanted to make the shell explode, since relatively thin armor would stop the shower of shell fragments. They used a 3-inch thick deck atop the belt—the heaviest thickness possible because of the weight effect on stability—to cause all but the most steeply plunging shells to glance off. A splinter deck of 1.5-inch STS was located directly below the armor deck, protecting the vital spaces: at the "torpedo bulkhead" (the outboard extremity of the vital spaces) the splinter deck angled down to the lower edge of the belt sealing off the vital spaces.

This arrangement, far in advance of contemporary foreign design practice, was first adopted in the *Nevada* and *Oklahoma*, designed early in 1911 and laid down in 1913. *Arizona* was effectively an enlarged version of *Nevada*. Although the "all or nothing" idea was public knowledge by that time, no foreign navy was willing to adopt it. Only after actual experience had proved the limited value of medium armor did the Europeans and Japanese follow the U. S. lead. Another expression of the U.S. lead was that, alone among the great naval powers, the U. S. Navy found it unnecessary to change the armor arrangement—essentially that used in the *Arizona*—after the British and Germans experienced the effect of plunging fire in the World War I Battle of Jutland.

The U. S. naval constructors were less fortunate in meeting the other major naval menace, the torpedo. In the earliest coal-fired American dreadnoughts, the coal was stored in deep bunkers along the sides of the ship. A torpedo exploding against the hull of the ship would expend its energy in pulverizing the coal. But the first "all or nothing" ship, *Nevada*, was also the first U.S. oil-burning battleship. The same Pacific strategy which demanded a large ship also required enormous cruising range which only the superior thermal content of oil could guarantee. But at the same time that meant abandoning the underwater protection that coal provided. Constructors feared that a torpedo exploding in oil tanks would set them on fire; they were wrong, but no experiments were made to test the theory. Instead, oil tanks were confined to the double-bottom of the ships and the coal was replaced by an armor bulkhead set inboard from the skin of the ship. In theory, the energy of a torpedo explosion would dissipate in the space between the side of the ship and the "torpedo bulkhead," and the last force of the explosion would go into denting that bulkhead. In fact, when the system was actually tested in mock-ups in 1914—with the ships it was to protect already under construction—the tests showed that the failing force of the explosion was enough to cave in the bulkhead. By that time it was too late to do much about it, although tests continued for the benefit of later ships.

The final solution was a "sandwich" of oil-filled "shock absorber" compartments and empty compartments (now called liquid-loaded and void) to take up the force of explosion, with the empty compartments inboard and outboard of the oil-filled compartments. The empty compartments near the side of the ship dispersed explosive energy, while those inboard were to take up leakage of oil from the shock-absorber compartments. This system required considerable space between the sides of the ship and the spaces to be protected, and so could be fitted only if space was made for it. That was exactly what was done in the reconstruction of the *Arizona;* the side of the ship was moved

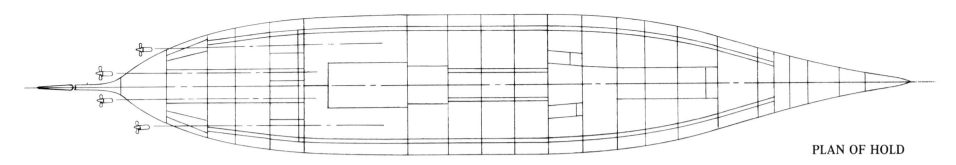

PLAN OF HOLD

Plan of HOLD *showing compartmentation, torpedo defense system, and shafting for the* BB *38 and* BB *39 class battleships as originally built.*

outward by installing an external bulge (or torpedo blister) and space was made in the boiler rooms by using more compact boilers.

Despite all the attention paid to protection, the published weight of armor in the *Arizona*—8,072 tons—seems low in comparison to that of contemporary foreign ships. That is because in U. S. practice the nominal "armor weight" included only the vertical armor—belt, turrets, barbettes and conning tower. Deck armor was counted as structural steel and a part of the hull weight. This was not very misleading in an era of half-inch armor decks, but in the early design stage it was already evident that the ship would have 2,224 tons of main armored deck and 1,297 tons of splinter deck; further weights were invested elsewhere in the hull. Total armor weight thus came to about 12,500 tons, nearly 40 per cent of the "normal" or design displacement. This was far beyond British practice, and comparable to that of the Germans; a remarkable performance considering that the Germans did not have to contend with providing for the endurance of Pacific operations.

Propulsion Plant

The main propulsion machinery for *Arizona* was a conventional steam plant consisting of 12 boilers supplying steam to four sets of turbines. There were four propeller shafts with each set of turbines driving a shaft.

Engines

Arizona was a very early application for steam turbines and reduction gearing in the U. S. Navy. As originally completed, she was powered by eight Parsons turbines coupled directly to four propellers. Two HP turbines drove the inboard pair of shafts, to which two HP astern turbines could also be coupled. The two outboard shafts were driven by two LP turbines which contained stages for going astern. Two cruising (intermediate pressure) turbines could be coupled to the outboard shafts through a reduction gear, affording more economy at lower speeds.

Unfortunate experiences with the geared cruising turbines of *Arizona* and her sister caused the U. S. Navy to develop turbo-electric drive systems, and several battleships were later completed with that type of propulsion. Turbines operated most efficiently at very high speeds, but propellers are most efficient at relatively low speeds. Lower speed turbines are much larger and heavier, and still cause the propellers to turn at inefficiently high speeds, resulting in a considerable loss of efficiency in transmitting the power to the water. Although just as heavy, or heavier, turbo-electric systems overcame these problems. The turbo-electric system was composed of boilers supplying steam to turbines driving generators which were directly coupled to the turbines. The generators were wired to large electric motors which drove the propellers; the speed of the motors could be controlled and thus the speed of the propellers was also controlled. The Royal Navy had successfully used reduction gearing which could step down turbine speed more than 10 to 1, but the factor that led to the development of reduction gearing in the U. S. Navy was the desperate need to save weight in ships built under the restrictions of the Washington Naval Disarmament Treaty of 1922.

Engine Rooms

The turbines and reduction gears were located in two machinery rooms directly below the mainmast. The machinery rooms were separated by a pump room on the centerline which had a longitudinal wiring passage extending several feet downward from the overhead in the center of the space.

The flooding of any of these three compartments would cause a considerable list, but it was considered that counterflooding of some of the voids would quickly correct the list. Increased draft, greater displacement, and a reduction in speed were, however, consequences which had to be accepted.

15

Boilers

Twelve Babcock & Wilcox watertube boilers supplied steam to the turbines. The boilers were oil fired and had a total heating surface of 55,332 square feet. Fuel oil storage capacity was 2,332 tons and 313.5 tons of reserve feed water was also carried.

Firerooms

The boilers were paired in six firerooms located directly below the stack. The boilers were fitted side by side in each fireroom and the uptakes penetrated the third deck individually. The longitudinal wiring passage was continued forward through the firerooms to the forward dynamo room.

Auxiliary Machinery

For the time at which she was built, *Arizona* had a powerful electric plant. The U. S. Navy was quite unusual in its preference for electrical rather than steam or hydraulic drive in such auxiliary equipment as turret training gears, etc.; and of course considerable power was required merely to light the ship and maintain internal communications.

Electrical power was provided by four 300 KW, 240 volt turbo-generators. Two generators were fitted in each dynamo room. The forward dynamo room was located just forward of the firerooms and the after dynamo room was between the firerooms and the machinery rooms.

Early Alterations and Modifications

From the time of her commissioning, in October 1917, until her reconstruction, in 1929, many alterations and modifications were made to *Arizona*. No major change in her appearance was made and those physical and functional changes which were made were basically minor. During World War I, *Arizona* did not serve with the British Grand Fleet but most of her early alterations were made as a result of the experience gained by other battleships during operations with the British.

Armament

Arizona lost eight of her 5-inch/51 caliber guns. By 1918 the four most forward and the four most aft casemate guns had been removed. These positions had been extremely wet, even in modest weather, and the guns were diverted to arm merchant ships for defense against submarine attack.

In view of wartime experience and the increasing threat of aircraft attack, the antiaircraft battery was doubled to eight 3-inch/50 caliber guns in 1923. The four additional guns were fitted two on each side of the forecastle deck adjacent to the bridge.

Fire Control

The secondary armament required fire control equipment, just as did the main battery. It was soon recognized that fire control stations had to be away from the noise and smoke of the individual guns in order to concentrate on attacking destroyers. The Royal Navy originated special director controls for this purpose, and the U.S. Navy operating with the British Grand Fleet in World War I soon adopted them.

After World War I, the secondary directors of U. S. battleships appeared as short cylinders protruding from the forecastle deck amidships just forward of the break. That location was not ideal and

they were relocated atop the tripod masts in the director towers during reconstruction.

After World War I, a 20-foot coincidence rangefinder was mounted on the bridge and a 12-foot instrument was fitted atop turret No. 3 between two of the 3-inch antiaircraft guns. An optical rangefinder's "base" was the distance between the two telescope lenses at the ends of the arms—the broader the base, the greater the accuracy.

Bridge

The small open bridge was removed and replaced by a larger, enclosed pilot house and chart room with windows and small open wings. It was built between the conning tower and the forward mast supported by struts from the superstructure deck. The new bridge was still crowded and somewhat cramped, but was a considerable improvement over the old one.

Masts

The structure of the cages was not altered but practically all of the equipment which they supported was modified or rebuilt and relocated to a different position on the mast. The spotting tops were enclosed from the weather and fitted with windows all around which could be lowered during battle. This new arrangement afforded the spotters and their equipment considerable protection over the old positions. The torpedo control platforms were enlarged and also enclosed with windows all around. The platforms were raised to about mid-height on each cage which gave a commanding view of approaches to the ship. The searchlight platforms were relocated above the torpedo control stations in groups of four as before. New yards were fitted and new antenna

supports were installed to support the wires of her new radio and communications gear.

Aircraft

Launching light fighter aircraft from platforms built onto the tops of battleship turrets had been successfully pioneered by the British during World War I. The turrets were pointed into the relative wind, and, with the ship moving at near-maximum speed, the small aircraft took off with little or no run. After the war ended, the U.S. Navy acquired 6 British and 22 French-built fighters with which to conduct similar operations. The first flight was made on 9 March 1919 at Guantanamo Bay, Cuba, from a platform over the forward superfiring turret of USS *Texas*, by a Sopwith Camel.* In July, 1919, the Secretary of the Navy ordered eight battleships equipped with aircraft platforms. On *Arizona* and *Pennsylvania* the after platform shared a turret top with two 3-inch AA guns.

The platforms were only marginally successful: only very small airplanes could be launched, and then only under ideal conditions; and they could not return to the ship. If land were not nearby, the airplane would have to ditch at the end of its flight. Nor was the single seater very useful for anything beyond air defense; for spotting or scouting the airplanes had to be large enough to carry an observer, and it had to be recoverable. Hence the development of catapults to launch large floatplanes. The first type, the trainable Mark A-1 compressed air catapult normally mounted on the fantail, made its first launch (of a Vought VE-7) from USS *Maryland* 24 May 1922. Earlier that year research on a more powerful gunpowder-charged catapult had begun,

* Ship's Data 6 USS Texas, p. 18.

Spotting planes were carried by all United States battleships. These "eyes of the fleet" float planes greatly extended the effective range of the main battery. This rendering shows Arizona's three SOC aircraft circa 1938. They are units of VO(observation squadron) One.

The flying-off platform is shown fully assembled, in photo at left, ready for flight operations and disassembled, in right photo, for normal operations. A Navy Nieuport is aboard. In the triple sleeve mounting of Arizona's *guns, elevation and depression was in unison. The flying-off platform consisted of two separate sections, one attached to the turret roof and one secured to the gun barrels. This arrangement allowed the guns to be elevated during battle operations without striking down the section over the gun barrels.*

Aircraft Types Used by USS *Arizona* (BB39)	
Year Designation	*Type*
1919 Sopwith Camel	Fighter, w/o floats, platform launch
1919 Nieuport 28	Fighter, w/o floats, platform launch
1919 Harriot HD-2	Fighter, w/o floats, platform launch
1920 Vought VE-7H	Floatplane, fighter-observation
1926 Vought FU-1	Floatplane, fighter-observation
1930 Vought O3U Corsair	Floatplane, fighter-observation
1936 Curtis SOC Seagull	Convertible, float/land observation
1940 Vought-Sikorsky OS2U Kingfisher	Convertible, float/land observation

the first test of which was carried out in 1924. Because it required no air line, the powder catapult could be mounted on a turret top without weakening the turret structure. Powder catapults replaced the compressed air types during the modernizations of the late twenties and early thirties; in a few cases they were mounted before modernization.

The VE-7 was a sturdy design dating from 1918. By 1926, *Arizona* was carrying two of the later Vought UO-1C biplanes, the Navy's last "wood-and-wire" type. A single seat fighter version, the FU-1, was developed to give the battleships some independent defensive power, but only twenty were bought and they saw only limited use. During the late twenties and into the thirties battleships were occasionally seen carrying the odd-looking Loening OL-series amphibians, whose fuselage merged with the main (centerline) float; these were the largest aircraft flown from battleship catapults until late in World War II. The last aircraft *Arizona* flew prior to her modernization were a pair of Vought O2U-1s, the first of a long line of outstanding designs named "Corsair" by the manufacturer. The Corsairs of 1927 were the first U. S. Navy observation planes to carry defensive armament, a single fixed machine gun firing forward and a pair of "flexible" machine guns on a mounting ring for the observer.

Arizona *lies at anchor in Guantanamo Bay, Cuba, 1 January 1920. The forward sections of her flying-off platforms are removed and their lower clamp supports can be seen on the gun barrels of turrets No. 2 and No. 3.*

In this 1921 photo of Arizona *at Lynn Haven Roads, angle deflection markings have been added to the superfiring turrets. The director control for the secondary battery can be seen in the form of short cylindrical houses; one is visible just abaft her boats and another is next to the bridge, barely visible. Note the 12-foot rangefinders atop the charthouse and turret No. 3.*

A compressed air catapult was mounted on Arizona's quarterdeck late in the twenties; it replaced the two turret-top flying-off platforms which had been less than successful. Two of the four secondary battery directors are visible in this view.

RECONSTRUCTION

The Washington Naval Limitations Treaty

The treaty defined the life of a battleship as 20 years after the date of completion. Construction could begin on a replacement after this lapse of time and the old ship was to be retired after completion of its replacement. By this provision, *Arizona* would be placed out of service about 1940 when her replacement was scheduled to be completed.

The treaty took into account the experience gained in the naval actions and with new weapons employed in the World War. It was accepted that certain improvements were necessary in existing capital ships in order to bring them up to current standards, primarily in regard to protection. Existing capital ships were permitted an increase in displacement of up to 3,000 tons for the inclusion of features against the effects or aerial bombing, plunging gunfire and underwater explosion.

Finally, a holiday in the construction of new capital ships was declared for a period of ten years, until the end of 1931. The British, however, were allowed to build two ships in order to bring them up to allowable treaty strength.

As soon as the treaty came into effect two actions were begun: the demilitarization and scrapping of those ships to be disposed of and the planning of the modernization of those ships that were to be retained. The Bureaus of Construction and Repair and Steam Engineering began feasibility studies which culminated in the contract plans for those ships to be rebuilt.

The initial effort was placed on the oldest ships since they would be the first replaced and taken out of service. The work was to be done in succession and in July 1924 the Boston Navy Yard began work on *Florida* (BB30) and *Utah* (BB31) followed by *Wyoming* (BB32) and *Arkansas* (BB33) at the Philadelphia Navy Yard. *New York* (BB34) and *Texas* (BB35) were assigned to the Norfolk Navy Yard and *Nevada* (BB36) and *Oklahoma* (BB37) were rebuilt at the Philadelphia Navy Yard during 1927 to 1929. Finally, on 25 February 1929, the reconstruction of *Pennsylvania* (BB38) and *Arizona* (BB39) was authorized by Congress and the work was assigned to the Norfolk Navy Yard.

The major items to be accomplished were: an increase in deck armor thickness for protection against aerial bombs and plunging shell fire, an increase in the torpedo and mine protection systems, new aircraft with their launching and recovery equipment, an increase in elevation (and thus range) of the main battery guns and modernization of fire control equipment, installation of a heavy antiaircraft battery, partially raise the secondary battery to higher locations, and generally upgrade the ships' ventilation and piping systems.

Two periscopes emerge from the top of turret No. 2, and one rises from the conning tower, in this 2 March 1931 view of the newly reconstructed Arizona. *Note the new enclosed bridge structure and the 5-inch/51 cal. and three 5-inch/25 cal. guns on each side of the superstructure (0-1 Level) deck.*

Hull

The most extensive work was to widen the hull. The 97' 0½" beam as originally built was increased to 106' 2¾" by the addition of a 4' 7⅜" bulge on each side of the ship. This was the maximum beam allowed for passage through the Panama Canal. The displacement was increased accordingly, allowing more weight to be carried at any draft, thus providing buoyancy to balance off the weight of the new armament and equipment being added. The bulge also added to the side protective system and insured a minimum loss of armored freeboard.

Although the shaft horsepower was increased during modernization (see MACHINERY section) the bulges altered the hull form and displacement resulting in a reduction in speed from 21.0 knots to 20.7 knots.

Machinery

The earliest schemes made use of new boilers and turbo-electric drive originally intended for ships scrapped under the treaty. The older coal-fired ships received priority for reconstruction, being considered inoperable unless their boilers were replaced. When Arizona was rebuilt in 1929–1931 the results were extensive, but not as radical as the gutting which had been proposed in 1922.

Boilers

Six new Bureau Express, three-drum boilers replaced the original twelve boilers. One was fitted in each fireroom where formerly two were installed side by side. The space savings allowed room for additional anti-torpedo protection (see ARMOR & PROTECTION section). An air lock was provided and the firerooms were pressurized for the new boilers.

The uptakes were in the same relative location and few alterations were required in way of the decks, keeping the armor penetration to a minimum. One stack was required as before; it was located slightly aft of the former stack in order to accommodate the enlarged bridge area and the uptakes were trunked accordingly in the new casing.

Engines

Reconstruction also involved the upgrading of Arizona's engines. The desperate need to reduce weight, under the terms of the treaty, forced the development of more efficient turbines and reduction gears and the abandonment of turbo-electric propulsion by the U. S. Navy. In part, Arizona benefited from this new technology.

The former HP turbines were replaced by newer geared units of slightly higher output. Although it was recognized that space and weight

---

* The idea that there was no point in making ships faster was by no means universal in 1930. When Japan reconstructed her battleships, a great deal of their effort was expended on their hulls and machinery to increase their speed. Even as late as 1941, this effort by the Japanese was largely unappreciated in the U. S. Navy.

could have been found for more powerful engines, there was little point seen in any increase in speed: the U. S. Navy thought 21 knots to be quite adequate.* The weight might better go into protection. Thus the power requirement for new engines was only that they balance off the increased resistance of the bulge. A significant benefit, of course, was far greater efficiency resulting in nearly tripled range on approximately twice the fuel supply.

Auxiliary Machinery

The four turbogenerators were upgraded to 400 KW each, in view of the great variety of added loads: cranes for aircraft, directors, etc., even more laundry equipment for the crew. Had Arizona survived Pearl Harbor, power loads would have further increased with the installation of light power-operated AA weapons and radar. By 1945, Arizona's surviving sister, Pennsylvania, had two additional 750 KW generators added bringing her total capacity to 3100 KW.

Fuel Storage

The fuel carrying capacity of Arizona was greatly increased during her reconstruction from 2,332 tons to 4,630 tons with provision for carrying up to 6,180 tons if necessary.

Oil was originally carried in the inner bottom tanks and tanks of the side protection system were kept void—the designers fearing that a torpedo hit in an oil-filled tank would set it ablaze. This was not the case, but for some reason no experiments were made to test the theory.

Oil was now stored in the two inner side tanks with a void buffer on either side (see TORPEDO DEFENSE SYSTEM below). With the newer, more efficient turbines and the additional fuel storage capacity, Arizona's cruising radius increased from 4,750 to 13,600 nautical miles at 15 knots. This considerably increased her capability for operations in the Pacific.

Now that more inner bottom tanks were available for liquid storage, the amount of reserve boiler feed water was increased proportionately with the remaining capacity going to potable water.

Armor and Protection

Two of the most important considerations of the rebuilding were providing for additional protection against plunging shellfire and torpedo attack. The addition of the bulge provided extra stability allowing weight to be put into deck armor and the transverse width it added formed another tank in the torpedo defense system.

Additional Armor

The major weight added was in deck and turret-top armor, officially (as per the treaty) intended as protection against aerial bombs. Of course, it also gave additional protection against long range plunging shellfire. Two inches of armor were added to the three already in place on the protective deck covering the top of the armor belt. An inch was also added to the turret tops. It should be noted, however, that the total

The newly modernized battleship at the Norfolk Navy Yard, 2 March 1931. She is complete except for the .50 cal. antiaircraft machine guns which would later occupy the platforms on both masts, and a catapult has not yet been mounted atop turret No. 3, although the boat cranes have been lengthened to serve it. The old cage masts have been replaced by tripods and topped with new three level fire control towers; the lowest level controlled the secondary battery and the upper two levels controlled and spotted for the main battery. The searchlight platform on the funnel proved unsatisfactory and the lights were later dispersed to platforms on the masts.

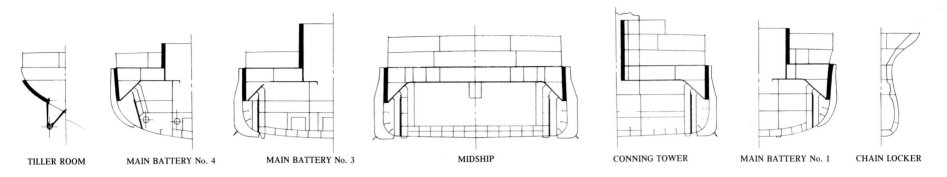

| TILLER ROOM | MAIN BATTERY No. 4 | MAIN BATTERY No. 3 | MIDSHIP | CONNING TOWER | MAIN BATTERY No. 1 | CHAIN LOCKER |

The midship and type sections of the BB 38 *and* BB 39 *class battleships as reconstructed and modernized during 1929-1931. For details of armor, see* GENERAL DATA.

of five inches of deck armor on the protective deck was by no means equivalent to a single layer of plate five inches thick. All of this armor was taken from supplies originally ordered for the ships cancelled in 1922.

Torpedo Defense System

The addition of the bulge provided substantial widening of the side protective system. The addition of another skin and tank considerably increased resistance to torpedo damage because it would have to occur much farther from the ship's vitals.

The new system consisted of four tanks: the outboard tank, formed by the bulge, was kept void, a new bulkhead was added in the former large outboard tank forming two new tanks which were oil-filled, and the former inboard tank which formed the boundary of the vitals at the holding bulkhead was kept void also. Space saved by the installation of

new boilers allowed an additional void tank to be fitted in way of the boiler rooms. In this area the inboard void became oil filled resulting in the following arrangement going inboard: void, liquid, liquid, liquid, void. This arrangement provided extra fuel oil service tanks adjacent to the firerooms. If turbo-electric propulsion had been installed as originally planned in 1922, the saving in space would have made it possible to extend the additional inboard void through the length of the engine rooms as well.

In theory, the numerous bulkheads of the system were flexible enough to deflect under gas pressure allowing the material to stretch and absorb energy before failure. The liquid was to stop fragments and splinters caused by an explosion. Damage and distortion would decrease as it proceeded inboard to the holding bulkhead which was intended to deform inboard but not tear. The new boilers were installed to clear the expected distortion of the holding bulkhead.

Plan of HOLD *showing compartmentation, torpedo defense system, and shafting for the* BB 38 *class battleships as modernized 1929-1931.*

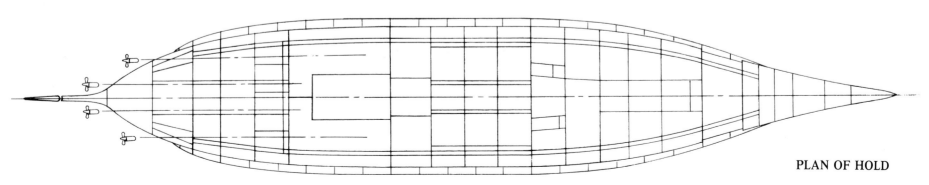

PLAN OF HOLD

Arizona *as outfitted in 1921.*

Standard– Light Gray Systems(later Haze Gray):
  Light gray on all horizontal and vertical surfaces except
  decks. Dark blue-gray on all decks.

Arizona *as outfitted in December 1941.*

Measure 14—Ocean Gray System:
  Ocean gray on hull and all superstructure masses. Haze
  gray on masts, yards and towers above level of
  superstructure masses. Deck blue on all decks.

Rendering by Alan B. Chesley/ Copyright © 1978 by FRA Br. 46
PRINTED IN U.S.A.

*Arizona as outfitted during her last overhaul period at the
Puget Sound Navy Yard, June 1941.*

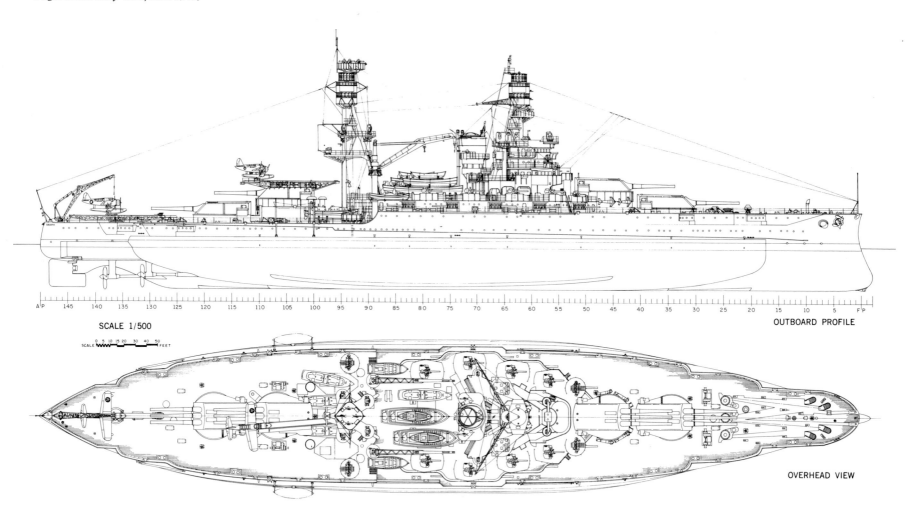

SCALE 1/500

OUTBOARD PROFILE

OVERHEAD VIEW

Drawing by Alan B. Chesley/Copyright © 1978 by FRA Br. 46

USS ARIZONA BASIC CONFIGURATIONS

Arizona as outfitted 1918

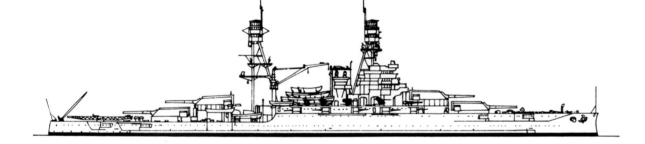

Arizona as outfitted 1931

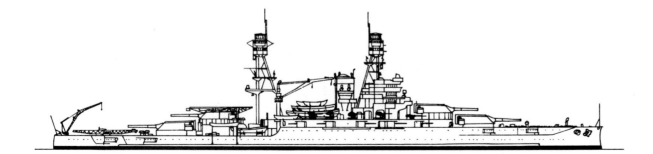

Arizona as outfitted 1936

SCALE 1/1200

0   50   100   200

Arizona's *sister ship,* Pennsylvania, *in an* ABSD (Advanced Base Sectional Dock) *for maintenance and painting somewhere in the Southwestern Pacific. Her rig suggests that the time is early 1943.*

Armament

When *Arizona*'s time for modernization came, several basic changes in naval tactics had occurred. The development and use of aircraft with the fleet had forever altered the standard "line of battle" techniques. The battle fleets had to be much more flexible in regard to both offensive and defensive operations.

Aircraft had provided a new means of spotting gunfire, extending battle ranges well beyond the horizon, and work was begun to extend the range of the main battery guns. On the other hand, aircraft provided a new means of attacking the battle line, and work was begun to develop both long range and close in antiaircraft armament.

Main Battery, 14-Inch/45 Caliber

By extending the visual range of the ship with spotting aircraft, it became worthwhile for the Bureau of Ordnance to develop a new and more powerful propelling charge for the 14-inch guns and increase the maximum elevation of the main battery from 15 to 30 degrees. The combination extended the range to 34,000 yards or almost twice the original range.

Except for the modification of the gun clearance holes in the face plates, the four triple turrets mounting the twelve 14-inch/45 caliber guns appeared as before. Some internal changes were required in order to accommodate the new travel of the breeches at maximum elevation.

This close-aboard view shows two 14-inch triple turrets as mounted in Arizona. *This photo is actually of* Arizona's *sister, the* Pennsylvania, *taken in the late thirties.*

All three guns in each turret were mounted together on a single slide. Note how the interrupted-screw breeches opened downward to provide clearance in the very limited space. In this type of triple mounting in one slide, all guns elevated and depressed together. This is one of the eight mounts built for the Arizona *and* Pennsylvania, *shown on test at the Naval Proving Ground.*

The term caliber refers to the length of the gun expressed in units of its bore, or the internal diameter of the barrel. Thus the barrel of a 14-inch/45 caliber gun is 45 × 14 inches in length, or 630 inches (52.5 feet) overall. Each gun was some 46 inches in outside diameter at the breech and weighed over 70 tons.

The gun tubes were "rifled" to improve accuracy; spiral grooves in the barrel imparted a spin to the projectile giving it a right hand twist of one revolution for each 37.3 feet of travel.

Every shot fired through the barrel eroded the liner, so that the gun required a new "liner" or innermost tube every 175 rounds. The ship carried about one hundred rounds of ammunition per gun, therefore, in order to be constantly maintained in a battle-ready condition the guns were relined every 75 rounds. This allowed very little margin for target practice, so special low-velocity target shells were developed. These fired at only 1,935 ft/sec (vs. 2,600) which was equivalent in gun wear to only 10% of a full AP round. Later in the thirties a HC shell was developed for shore bombardment. The explosive in the HC shell was not as dense as the nearly solid steel of the AP shell and the reduction in shell weight amounted to only 78% of the wear of the AP shell.

Secondary Battery, 5-Inch/51 Caliber

The secondary armament in U.S. battleships underwent a fundamental change in concept between World War I and World War II. The threat

Arizona *completed her modernization with eight 5-inch/25 cal. antiaircraft guns installed and positions for eight .50 cal. machine guns; the latter mount was not completely developed for shipboard use at that time. In theory, the heavier 5-inch would discourage high-altitude bombers and the .50 cal., the strafers. Neither appeared to answer the problem of dive bombers.*

The 5-inch/25 cal. guns in open mounts were vulnerable to strafing and splinters; in the summer of 1941, shields were developed for them. The new protection against splinters consisted of fixed plating on the deck with working-circle clearance, and shields on the mount which rotated with the gun. At the time of the attack on Pearl Harbor, all battleships were fitted with fixed protection but few had the rotating shields on the guns. This 26 February 1942 view of Pennsylvania *shows both modifications, which had been scheduled for* Arizona. *Note the details of the 5-inch/25 cal. breech mechanism and the fuze-setting rack on the left hand side of the mount. The MK 28 director, one on each side of the bridge, controlled the 5-inch/25 cal. guns.*

of destroyers rushing in on the battle line to make a torpedo attack was becoming secondary to the threat of torpedo and bombing attack from aircraft.

In practice, the 5-inch/51 caliber guns were mounted so low that they were useless in almost any sea state. During modernization, *Arizona*'s secondary battery was completely altered. Only twelve of the 5-inch/51's were retained: ten were moved one deck higher and enclosed in a new superstructure deckhouse, and two were placed atop the new superstructure deckhouse abreast the conning tower.

The reduction of the number of guns in the secondary battery made weight available for additional antiaircraft armament. Even if the full impact of airpower had been realized, it is doubtful that the Navy would have abandoned the anti-destroyer gun for more antiaircraft defense; after all, the Japanese had invested heavily in large destroyers with heavy torpedo batteries. When she was lost, *Arizona*'s armament still included a large component of obsolete secondary guns.

Antiaircraft Battery, 5-Inch/25 Caliber

Eight of the new 5-inch/25 caliber guns were fitted, four on each side, atop *Arizona*'s new superstructure deckhouse. They were arranged to cover the largest arc of fire possible for both air and surface targets. The new gun was developed to fill the need for an antiaircraft gun of larger caliber with a high rate of fire. It was a semi-automatic, double purpose weapon, which could be used against surface targets as well as aircraft. The gun could be moved rapidly in both elevation and train and its fuze setter was mounted to the left and aft of the breech on the gun platform which was attached to the gun carriage.

Antiaircraft Battery, 1.1-Inch Mount

The 1.1-inch machine gun was designed as an intermediate range weapon to supplement the 5-inch/25 antiaircraft gun and the .50 caliber machine gun. The gun was intended to take up the fire on a target which was too close in for effective firing by the 5-inch and not yet within range of the .50 caliber guns. A quadruple mounting was chosen for the gun in order to give it a satisfactory rate of fire. The original mounts were manually operated, but power drives were later developed to increase efficiency.

Prototypes of the mount appeared as early as 1931, but the gun was not ready for production until 1934. Production proceeded at a slow rate until the Emergency AA Improvement Program was initiated in the spring of 1940. The program called for four 1.1-inch gun mounts to be installed in each of the Pacific Fleet battleships.

Arizona was scheduled to receive her allowance of 1.1-inch mounts early in 1942. During her refit of June 1941 at the Puget Sound Navy Yard, foundations, ammunition hoists, and ready service lockers were installed—the mounts were to be delivered to Pearl Harbor later and dropped in place. The exposed pair of 5-inch/25 guns on the superstructure deckhouse abreast the conning tower were removed and two foundations were fitted in their place; a second pair of foundations was fitted on the main deck just aft of the break, one on each side of the mainmast. At the time of her loss, these positions were empty.

Antiaircraft Battery—.50 Caliber Mount

In the 1920s, it was recognized that aircraft strafing a ship presented a threat which neither of the 5-inch guns could counter. The .50 caliber heavy machine gun was developed from the original Browning water-cooled gun used so effectively during the First World War. It had a high

The 1.1-inch machine gun was intended to counter the threat of the dive bomber; but it proved difficult to produce and unreliable in service. The fleet antiaircraft modernization (King Board) program of 1940–1941 called for four quadruple 1.1-inch mounts per battleship, with an interim battery of four 3-inch/50 cal. guns in their positions. Arizona had the positions, but neither weapon at the time of her loss. This 1.1-inch gun mount is aboard Pennsylvania at the Mare Island Navy Yard, 26 February 1942.

The .50 cal. machine gun was intended to discourage strafers. With the development of heavier and faster aircraft, it proved too light to be effective unless a high concentration of fire could be attained; deck space available made it impractical to mount the gun in the numbers required for effective concentration of fire. The gun continued to be used on some older ships well after the new 20mm mounts were being installed.

rate of fire and provided fast pointing which proved very effective against dive bombing and other forms of close-in attack during tests conducted in the mid-1930s.

During reconstruction, platforms were provided high on both tripod masts for mounting the .50 caliber guns. Although officially on the ship's allowance list for modernization, the guns were not ready until about 1933.

Torpedo Tubes

As originally designed, *Arizona* was to have four torpedo tubes—she completed with only two. The tubes were mounted athwartship below the water line for broadside firing. By the time the ship was reconstructed, the battle ranges had been extended so far by the modifications to the main battery guns and ammunition, that the tubes were considered useless. In addition, the space required by the torpedo rooms below the waterline constituted a threat to the side protection system by interrupting its continuity. It was suggested that the torpedoes be relocated above decks in tube banks, but in the end they were removed and the space integrated into the side protection system.

Had Arizona *not been destroyed at Pearl Harbor, she would have been refitted similar to the interim changes shown in this February 1942 photograph of her sister ship* Pennsylvania. *Splinter protection was provided for the 5-inch/25 and light antiaircraft guns. Note the mixed antiaircraft machine gun Battery - the pair of 1.1-inch quad guns in tubs supported from the main deck, the 20mm guns halfway up the mainmast, and the .50 cal. guns in the bird bath.*

Superstructure Deck

Alterations in the superstructure area were extensive. A new superstructure deck was fitted on the upper deck (forecastle deck) extending from barbette No. 2 aft to the break of the deck. The remaining ten 5-inch/51s from the secondary battery were relocated in casemate mountings in the new deckhouse. The casemates also served as accommodation for the crew: sleeping was in hammocks which were struck down and stowed during the day. The space between the casemates housed the bakery forward, the crew's galley aft, and the foundry and metal shop in the center around the uptakes. The eight new 5-inch/25 double purpose guns were fitted atop the new deckhouse, four on each side, and the new bridge enclosure occupied the space between barbette No. 2 and the stack. The ship's boats were nested aft of the stack and were serviced by two new cranes which were located on the main deck just aft of the upper deck (*see* SHIP'S BOATS *section*).

Bridge

Arizona's bridge was greatly enlarged and modernized. A flag bridge was fitted above the superstructure deck and an emergency cabin platform was over the flag bridge with a chart house and sea cabins for the flag and chief of staff. The next level up was the navigating bridge with an enclosed pilot house, the top of which was the range finder platform.

After modernization, *Arizona* differed somewhat from her sister *Pennsylvania* in the bridge area. *Pennsylvania* was fitted as a fleet flagship while *Arizona* served as a divisional flagship. *Pennsylvania* had an extra level built onto her conning tower for the fleet commander and his staff: during battle they had an almost completely unobstructed view through 300 degrees.

Director Towers and Masts

The old cage masts were landed and new tripods of equal height were fitted in the same location as the cages. The foremast was stepped on the second deck and the mainmast on the third deck.

New fire control systems were fitted as evidenced by the large multi-level fire control "fighting tops" which enclosed the tops of the new tripod masts. The highest level was a circular cupola enclosing the main battery director, below it was an angular two story enclosure carrying the main battery control station on the upper level and a secondary battery control station on the lower level with secondary battery directors on each side. The "fighting tops" fitted to the foremast and the mainmast were identical. This arrangement elevated the main battery director station, main battery control station, and secondary battery control station to 111', 107', and 99' above the 28' 10" design water line respectively. The main battery range finders were relocated to the top of the new bridge structure and to a platform on the new tripod mainmast.

Hatches and vertical ladders provided access between levels in the "fighting tops" and each had an escape hatch leading to its roof; the reason for the top being stepped. In action, all windows slid down into frames to improve visibility and reduce the hazard of glass splinters.

Both tripods carried topmasts with small yardarms that were retractable for clearance. A large yardarm was fitted to the sides of the lower level of each "fighting top." The yards and masts supported the flag hoists and usual array of communication equipment. Concentration dials were fitted on each mast but bearing scales were eliminated from the turrets.

Accommodation

Crew requirements were altered during modernization, but most enlisted men still slept in hammocks. After her June 1941 refit at the Puget Sound Navy Yard, Arizona had accommodations for 2,037 men, nearly twice as many as were required to man her when she was completed.

Aircraft

During modernization, Arizona had her compressed air catapult on the fantail replaced by a trainable powder type (P Mk VI), and a fixed powder catapult (P Mk IV Mod I) was installed atop Number Three turret, training with the turret. Aircraft were normally stowed on the catapults, no enclosed hangars being provided. There was a single aircraft crane on the fantail, the turret catapult being served by the main boat cranes.

Aircraft were recovered at sea by having the ship make a wide sweeping turn into the wind to create a calm "slick" into which the pilot could land. He would then taxi toward the moving ship and on to a sledlike device trailed from the recovery crane. The sled was covered by a rope net, and hooks on the bottom of the aircraft's main float would catch in the net as the throttle was cut back. The recovery crew then lowered a hook from the crane for the observer to secure in a lifting sling at the center of the upper wing; and finally, plane and sled could be hoisted aboard. The elaborate procedure clearly required great skill on the part of aircrew, crane crew, and ship's conning officer. Nonetheless, it was never improved upon, and the need for it lapsed only when radar and helicopters rendered fixed-wing shipborne observation aircraft obsolete.

After her modernization, Arizona normally carried three Vought O3U Corsair spotting planes, although a fourth, painted blue, might occasionally be embarked for the Admiral's use. In 1935 the Corsairs were replaced by the Curtiss SOC Seagull, the Navy's last biplane spotting aircraft. Arizona carried three Seagulls of Observation Squadron One until she returned to the West Coast late in 1940 for overhaul. On her return to Pearl Harbor (July 1941), she was equipped with her final spotter complement of three OS2U-2 Kingfisher monoplanes. The elegant Kingfisher replaced Seagulls in all Pacific Fleet battleships, but the sturdy Seagull continued in front-line service aboard cruisers until nearly the end of World War II.

Pennsylvania *illustrates the radar configuration planned for* Arizona; *an air search set (which would have been a SC rather than the CXAM-1 shown here) and a MK 3 main battery fire control set forward of it. At this time the MK 4 dual purpose fire control radar had not yet appeared. Note the addition of extensive splinter protection, the 1.1-inch quad machine guns, and many 20mm machine guns, some on new platforms.*

Plans for the reconstruction of Pennsylvania *and* Arizona *were drawn up before the war.* Pennsylvania *was refitted in the fall of 1942 to a somewhat more austere standard than originally planned, but nonetheless suggests what was planned for* Arizona.

Final Configuration

In December 1941, *Arizona*'s appearance had changed very little since her reconstruction. She had overhauls at the Puget Sound Navy Yard during January 1934, March 1936, September 1937, April 1939, and June 1941. The alterations and modifications made during the last period were intended to bring her up to a readiness for war and are described below.

The exposed pair of 5-inch/51 caliber guns, on the superstructure deck abreast the conning tower, were removed and the positions to be filled with the new 1.1-inch quadruple machine gun mounts being manufactured. Another pair of 1.1-inch mounts were to be installed on the main deck abreast the mainmast. Foundations, ballistic shields, ammunition hoists, and ready service lockers were installed for the mounts which were to be delivered early in 1942.*

The .50 caliber machine guns were relocated several times to improve their arc of fire. Originally, four were mounted on a platform on each mast. The four searchlights carried on the funnel were removed in 1939 and two of the .50 caliber guns from the mainmast replaced them. In 1941 the "birdbath" platform was fitted atop the director tower on the mainmast and filled with four .50 caliber guns; two from the foremast and two from the mainmast. This left two mounts on the foremast platform and two on the funnel platform. The former gun platform on the mainmast was fitted with four searchlights of uniform size.

*All Pacific Fleet battleships were to receive four 1.1-inch quadruple mounts. On some ships, like USS *Oklahoma*, 3-inch/50 caliber antiaircraft guns were installed on 1.1-inch foundations. *Arizona*'s foundations were empty on 7 December 1941.

Splinter protection was provided for the eight 5-inch/25 caliber guns mounted on the superstructure deck and similar protection was given to all .50 caliber machine guns in the upperworks.

New Mk 28 antiaircraft directors were installed which considerably improved the efficiency of the 5-inch/25 caliber guns. The directors were fitted at the range finder platform level of the bridge, which afforded sufficient sky arc coverage, and were supported from the superstructure deck by their heavy wiring tubes.

Arizona was scheduled to receive air search and fire control radar equipment early in 1942 or as soon as the equipment was available. Structural modifications had been made during her last overhaul and work was progressing on the installation of system components. The air search radar was to be the new SC type and the pedestal for its antenna can be seen atop the forward director tower in the photographs of the wreck. The Mk 3 fire control radar was to be installed for the main battery and its antenna was to be mounted atop the forward director tower also, just forward of the SC pedestal.

Planned Alterations

By 1939 when World War II began in Europe, *Arizona* had a mixed secondary battery of anti-destroyer and antiaircraft 5-inch guns. Inherently, the differing ballistics of the two guns made unified control against both surface and air targets difficult, but the Navy was unwilling to give up the anti-destroyer guns because of the large destroyers Japan had built with their heavy torpedo batteries. The solution adopted was the new double purpose 5-inch/38 caliber twin gun mount designed for the *North Carolina* class battleships.

In 1940 plans were drawn up for the reconstruction of *Pennsylvania* and *Arizona*, removing the mixed battery and incorporating the new 5-inch/38 caliber gun mount. Under these plans, the superstructure deck house was to be cut away and four of the new twin mounts fitted to each side, all on the forecastle deck. It was also planned to replace the 1.1-inch quadruple machine gun mounts (which were never installed) with the new 40mm Swedish Bofors quadruple machine gun mount then under development. Similarly, the .50 caliber machine guns were to be replaced with the new 20mm Swiss Oerlikons also under development. The Bofors and Oerlikons would have replaced the older guns on a one to one basis.

A somewhat similar conversion was actually carried out on *Pennsylvania*, except that the superstructure deck house was retained and the mainmast cut away for a new fire control platform. Presumably the light antiaircraft battery would have been expanded considerably during the war had *Arizona* survived the attack on Pearl Harbor; by 1945, *Pennsylvania* mounted one twin and ten quad 40mm gun mounts, and twenty-nine single and twenty-two twin 20mm gun mounts.

Had Arizona *survived the attack on Pearl Harbor, she would have been altered similar to this rendering. Note the SC air search and MK 3 fire control radar antennas, the MK 37 fire control directors and twin 5-inch/38 gun mounts, the 1.1-inch and 20mm machine guns, and the Measure 12 camouflage painting scheme.*

Arizona is in the foreground of this mid 1930s photograph of the Battle Force steaming away from the comera. Before World War II the Battle Force was the primary embodiment of United States sea power.

OPERATIONAL HISTORY

The USS *Arizona* served quite effectively as a battleship for a quarter century before her loss during the attack on Pearl Harbor, 7 December 1941. Her design was typical of the best American practice of the dreadnought period, and her career is typical of units of the Battle Fleet with which she operated between the wars. In that sense, her story is the story of the main strength of the U. S. Fleet between 1916 and 1941.

In March 1931, Soon after her recommissioning, Arizona *played host to President Hoover. President Hoover was aboard for the cruise to Puerto Rico in 1931. Above, the President and Secretary Hurley walk her quarterdeck; note the Vought 03U Corsairs on her catapult. In the photograph at right,* Arizona *flies the Presidential flag; note the empty platforms reserved for the installation of .50 cal. machine guns and, in both photographs, the early type of quarterdeck aircraft crane.*

After her commissioning, *Arizona* joined the Atlantic Fleet and remained in home waters during the first World War. Many of the older battleships joined the British Grand Fleet, but *Arizona*, being one of our first oil burners would have presented additional logistic problems and she was used for gunnery training off the east coast, after the Armistice she joined the Grand Fleet on 30 November 1918, remaining in British waters for only a short time. In May 1919, *Arizona* was ordered to Smyrna, Turkey, to protect American lives and property during the Greek occupation of that port. Later she transported the U.S. Consul-at-Large, L. E. Morris, to Constantinople, returning home to New York in July. She refitted at the New York Navy Yard and then became Flagship of Battleship Division 7, and Flagship of the entire Battle Force Atlantic Fleet (July and August, 1921).

By this time the Navy was already beginning to concentrate its fleet in the Pacific. *Arizona* joined the Pacific Fleet on 21 August 1921, remaining there for the remainder of her career, except for her reconstruction and a cruise to Puerto Rico. During the two decades of peace between the wars, the Battle Fleet exercised in annual Fleet Problems designed to test plans for a war which might one day be fought against Japan. Some of the Fleet Problems were prophetic: fleet actions including aircraft carriers with air attacts on Pearl Harbor and the Panama Canal. The Fleet also made numerous "show the flag" cruises, the most spectacular being the long cruise to Australia and New Zealand in 1925.

Arizona entering San Francisco Bay in the late 1930s flying the flag of a Rear Admiral in her role as Flagship, Battleship Division (Bat Div) One. The .50 cal. machine guns are in place on her masts.

As Japan expanded her forces in China in the late thirties, the Battle Fleet, including *Arizona*, was brought up to date and contingency plans for moving the main fleet base from San Diego to Pearl Harbor were formulated. The latter had the virtue of closeness to the probable battle area. It was thought that the Japanese would use their submarines and aircraft to shave away the American edge in number of battleships (15 to 10 in 1941); the closer the Fleet to Japanese waters, the less shaving would be possible before the main fleet engagement both sides expected.

BATTLESHIPS, BATTLE FORCE (SAN PEDRO)
WEST VIRGINIA—Flagship

BATTLESHIP DIVISION 1	BATTLESHIP DIVISION 2
ARIZONA—Flag	TENNESSEE—Flag
NEVADA	OKLAHOMA
PENNSYLVANIA—Fl. Flag	CALIFORNIA—Force Flag
Air Unit—Obs. Sq. 1–9 VOS	Air Unit—Obs. Sq. 2–9 VOS

BATTLESHIP DIVISION 3	BATTLESHIP DIVISION 4
IDAHO—Flag	WEST VIRGINIA—Flag
MISSISSIPPI	COLORADO
NEW MEXICO	MARYLAND
Air Unit—Obs. Sq. 3–9 VOS	Air Unit—Obs. Sq. 4–9 VOS

The Fleet was moved to Pearl Harbor on a temporary basis after the completion of Fleet Problem XXI in May 1940. Its value as a deterrent to the Japanese was so highly regarded in Washington that it was held there through 1941. Battleships and other units left Pearl harbor only on exercises or en route to refits.

Loss of the Arizona

Arizona is best remembered for the nature of her loss, perhaps the worst single naval disaster in our history and certainly the best known symbol of the attack on Pearl Harbor. Her loss was caused by exactly the weapon that the Navy had tried to protect her against during the 1929–1931 reconstruction: the aerial bomb.

The Battle Fleet was almost totally unprepared for the attack. By late 1941 war with Japan was considered imminent and studies had been made considering the various types of attack that could be launched, however, none of the studies had anticipated the exact nature of the attack or when it might come. The Japanese succeeded beyond their wildest dreams and could only have hoped that the carriers had been in harbor also.

In examining the damage to the Battle Fleet, consideration should be given to the conditions that prevailed in Pearl Harbor and aboard the ships in order to understand their lack of battle readiness. In many cases the final damage far exceeded that which could be expected during the course of normal battle operations at sea.

Arizona *at sea for gunnery practice, probably in the late 1930s. She still has her whaleboat and davits rigged on the side toward which her guns are trained, which suggests practice with subcaliber guns.*

Although the Battle Fleet was officially based at Pearl Harbor the base was still considered to be inadequate: lacking in services, air defense, repair and docking facilities, and personnel. Efforts were being made to strengthen the base as quickly as material and personnel became available. Units operated as much as possible preparing for war and many times routine maintenance was left to the week-end duty sections while in port. In many ships on 7 December 1941 doors and other closures were open, apparently for working parties, and items such as tools and cleaning gear were adrift.

The primary defense against aerial attack was provided by land based fighters. Because of the surprise nature of the attack, almost all aircraft capable of intercepting the attackers were either crippled or destroyed on the ground. The secondary defense against aerial attackers had to come from antiaircraft batteries on the ships and the limited shore installations. As with most United States battleships in 1941, Arizona was armed with eight 5-inch/25 cal. double purpose guns for long range firing and eight .50 cal. machine guns for close-in "last ditch" firing. The new intermediate range 1.1-inch quad. mounts were ordered for all battleships but only *Maryland* had them installed at the time of the attack. Although a respectable antiaircraft barrage was put up late during the attack,* antiaircraft defenses were inadequate.

*See photo, page 18, *Pearl Harbor Attack,*   FRA Br. 46.

The battleships were, therefore, forced to rely primarily on their passive defenses and the real confrontation was between the Japanese aerial torpedoes, armor piercing bombs, and light case bombs and the torpedo defense systems and deck armor of the battleships.

The exact cause of *Arizona*'s loss will probably never be known. A final analysis of the loss was prepared for the BuShips by CDR E. C. Holtzworth, USN on 31 October 1944. The analysis is quoted here and key frames from the film, Ref: (f), are shown:

ANALYSIS OF LOSS OF ARIZONA
Ref. (a) NYPearl ltr. C-L11-1/BB, NY10, Serial Y-02149, of 7 October, 1943 (War Damage Report)
   (b) C.O. ARIZONA ltr. of 17 December 1941 to Combatfor (Material Damage Report).
   (c) C.O. ARIZONA ltr. BB39/A16 of 7 December, 1941 (Action Report).
   (d) C.O. ARIZONA ltr. BB39/A9/l11-1 of 28 January, 1942 (Damage Report).
   (e) C.O. VESTAL ltr. AR4/L11-1/(066) of 11 December, 1941 (Action Report).
   (f) Roll of 35mm movie film, obtained through the Office of Strategic Services, of USS ARIZONA on the morning of 7 December, 1941— Photographer, Capt. Eric Haakensen

The references comprise the majority of important information accumulated regarding the loss of ARIZONA. Certain other action reports, notably those of WEST VIRGINIA, TENNESSEE, and MARYLAND, contain fragmentary

These frames from a motion picture film show the destruction of the Arizona; *aft of her is the bow of the* Nevada *and the badly listing masts of the* West Virginia *are visible forward of her in the first two shots. Photo 3 is very nearly the moment of impact of a bomb which struck the forecastle, after which the fireball of photos 4 was produced. This was followed by a jet of black smoke from her funnel, which begins in photo 5, and the beginning of smoke from the explosion forward. The fire appears to have spread very rapidly in the next three shots, and photo 9 appears to show the beginning of the magazine explosion which actually destroyed the ship. The remaining three photos show the progression of the holocaust. These shots span a total of approximately seven seconds.*

information of minor value. Reference (a) is a fairly extensive report of damage prepared by the Navy Yard, Pearl Harbor and is based on salvage and diving operations covering a period of approximately 22 months. Reference (f) actually shows the magazine explosion which resulted in the loss of ARIZONA. All these sources were used, as well as certain publications of the Army with respect to stability and characteristics of black powder and smokeless powder, in the following analysis:

SECTION I—NARRATIVE

1. On the morning of 7 December, 1941, ARIZONA was moored to interrupted quay "F-7," headed down channel, starboard side to Ford Island. Outboard of ARIZONA and pointed up channel was VESTAL. Immediately astern of ARIZONA was NEVADA at berth F-8. Immediately forward of ARIZONA at berth F-6 was TENNESSEE, moored starboard side to, and WEST VIRGINIA outboard of TENNESSEE, with both vessels being headed down channel. ARIZONA's bow was very close to TENNESSEE's stern—the distance being approximately 200 feet. The same distance separated the stern of the ARIZONA from the bow of NEVADA.

2. Depth of water was about 45 feet, and ARIZONA's drafts were 32'-6" forward and 33 feet aft. At 0755 all "X" doors and fittings should have been closed and reference (d) states that they were all closed with very few exceptions. Many

"Y" doors and fittings also were closed from the previous night. The majority of engineeing spaces were in condition "Z" and locked. Reference (d) further states that when the attack started, condition ZED was nearly set in turrets III and IV. There were no survivors from turrets I and II, and reference (d) believes that they probably were in condition ZED, or very nearly so. It appears that condition ZED was not completely set on and above the third deck and probably most of the third deck armored hatches were still open.

3. The attack started at 0755 with dive bombers over the Naval Air Station on Ford Island. At this time the measures referred to in paragraph 2 were started. Almost simultaneously a torpedo attack on battleship row occurred. The Commanding Officer of VESTAL, in reference (e), stated that at about 0820 a torpedo was seen to pass astern of the VESTAL and that this torpedo apparently hit the ARIZONA, whose bow extended about 100 feet beyond the stern of VESTAL. He further states that ARIZONA's forward magazine exploded. Reference (b) lists eight bomb hits on the vessel, one of which apparently was large and of the armor piercing type. This one was reported by reference (b) to have hit on the forecastle by No. II turret. In any event, the magazine explosion destroyed the ship almost completely forward of the foremast structure.

4. Reference (a) found evidence of only five bomb hits, all of which were aft of the foremast structure. At the same time the ship was so thoroughly broken up forward of the foremast structure that evidence of a heavy bomb hit in the vicinity of turret II would be certain to be completely obliterated. On the other hand the armor belt was substantially intact and Pearl Harbor found no apparent evidence of a torpedo hit on or just below the armor.

5. Times in all the references of the various sequences of events check reasonably well, that is, within 4 or 5 minutes. It appears that ARIZONA escaped torpedo damage during the initial torpedo attack which occurred at about 0800. It will be recalled that NEVADA was hit by a torpedo between 0800 and 0810, and that WEST VIRGINIA was torpedoed at about the same time. Following this attack the dive bombing attack on the battleship started. This was at about 0815-0820. All the references agree that the bombs which struck ARIZONA fell between 0815 and 0820. For example, it appears that WEST VIRGINIA was struck by bombs at about this time, as was TENNESSEE. It appears that the dive bombing continued from about 0810 to 0830 in this phase of the attack.

6. Reference (f), of which a 3" x 5" movie strip is available, comprises about 400 pictures taken at the rate of 24 per second. This dramatic movie footage was taken by Captain Eric Haakensen, a U. S. Navy Physician on board USS Solace.

Arizona as seen from Ford Island just after the attack with her oil burning furiously to produce masses of black smoke.

7. The first 45 of these pictures show the ARIZONA and VESTAL, and include the bow of NEVADA and the stern of WEST VIRGINIA. There seems to be no damage to ARIZONA in these pictures, but evidence of the fire on VESTAL's forecastle (she was struck by a bomb, apparently prior to 0820) is faintly visible. WEST VIRGINIA's mainmast is also in these pictures and shows a definite list, indicating that WEST VIRGINIA had already been torpedoed prior to the pictures. This is consistent with the time reported. Between pictures 45 and 46 the camera was apparently stopped for an indeterminate time. Picture 46 definitely shows an explosion on the bow of ARIZONA. It is estimated that picture 46 was taken within 0.5 sec. of the detonation. As the pictures proceed, the fire gets worse, finally engulfing the entire ship forward of the mainmast. This series continues until picture 208. Between pictures 46 and 208 the development of a jet of black smoke from ARIZONA's stack can be noted. It is this jet of black smoke which apparently gave rise to the rumor that a bomb went down her stack.

Battleships carried a great deal of oil: Arizona's wreck continued to burn all day. She was essentially undamaged aft, but her forepart was totally destroyed and her foremast toppled.

Salvage divers did not examine the armor gratings, but they were believed to be intact, although there was bomb damage both forword and to the port of the uptakes. These bombs unquestionably damaged the air intakes to the steaming fireroom. The smoke issuing from the stack was quite obviously the result of incomplete combustion rather than an explosion or fire. Beginning with the pictures in the vicinity of 106, the characteristics of the conflageration shown are somewhat similar to those of an oil fire. At various places between pictures 46 and 208 minor explosions on the forecastle of ARIZONA and possibly on the stern of TENNESSEE, can be seen.

8. Picture 208 definitely shows the magazine explosion in which the dense black smoke of the previous picture changes to white, and luminous objects can be seen. Toward the end of the reel the sagged forward structure becomes apparent, although the smoke and flame obscure the entire foremast structure in the series of pictures following 208. Picture 208 occurred approximately 7 seconds (24 frames per second) after the detonation shown in picture 46. There is no evidence that the camera was stopped at any time between pictures 46 and 208.

9. The above evidence leads to the conclusion that there was a bomb detonation on or about the forecastle, which caused a bad fire—involving in some manner oil from tanks forward of amidships. This fire spread rapidly over a large area and increased rapidly in intensity. It was followed in 7 seconds by a magazine explosion.

10. In examining the causes of the magazine explosion, characteristics of smokeless powder and black powder were investigated. Pertinent information from the Ordnance Safety Manual published 1 September, 1941 by the Office of the Chief of Ordnance, U.S. Army, are quoted below:

"Small amounts of unconfined smokeless powder burn with little smoke or ash and without explosion. When confined or in large quantities, the rate of burning increases with the temperature and pressure. Under certain conditions, with sufficient initiation, smokeless powder has been known to detonate."

"When smokeless powder is stored in magazines in containers or propelling charges, there is no evidence to indicate that fires will give rise to any unusual hazard."

"Cases in which pressures great enough to result in structural damage have occurred involved the burning or explosion of smokeless powder under circumstances not ordinarily encountered in the storage of the material in containers."

"There is, however, incontrovertible evidence that explosions of nitro-cellulose powders up to large sizes are capable of being orocagated from box to box when they are initiated by detonation of high explosive charges."

It can be concluded from the above conditions that smokeless powder is difficult to detonate as a result of fire.

With respect to the properties of black powder, the following pertinent information is quoted from the same manual:

"Black powder is regarded as one of the worst known explosive hazards. When ignited unconfined, it burns with explosive violence, and will explode if ignited under even slight confinement. It can be ignited easily by very small sparks, heat, and friction."

"Most black powder fires start from sparks, and ignition results in an explosion so quickly that no attempt can be made to fight the fire."

"Most explosions of black powder originate from sparks."

"Loose black powder is extremely dangerous."

It can be seen from the above that the ignition of black powder will almost inevitably result in an explosion.

11. From reference (a) the ARIZONA had on board her full allowance of smokeless powder, arranged three magazines on each side of the vessel between frames 31 and 48 on the first platform. These six magazines supply both turrets I and II. The black powder magazine is located on the first platform on the centerline between frames 37 and 39. It contained 1075 pounds of black powder. It will be realized that the black powder magazine is surrounded by the smokeless powder magazines.

12. After the magazine explosion occurred, reference (a) reports that exploded 5"/51 caliber powder cans were found along the beach on Ford Island—a distance of 350-400 feet on the starboard side of the vessel. The 5"/51 caliber powder magazines are located on the first platform aft of the 14-inch smokeless powder magazines and between frames 50 and 58, port and starboard.

13. There is no doubt that the smokeless powder magazines detonated. It is not clear, however, what initiated the smokeless powder detonation. A bomb detonation within the smokeless powder magazines presumably could cause a detonation, although smokeless powder as such is not an unusually severe hazard. The Army's experience indicates that it is difficult to detonate smokeless powder as the result of fire, unless confinement, temperature, pressure, and high density of loading are present. Our own war experience has indicated that an appreciable interval of time (longer than 7 seconds) is required for these factors to build up and create a mass detonation following a fire. Fire could reach the magazines through hatches left open on the third deck. There are five such hatches in the vicinity of barbettes 1 and 2, one of which is almost directly above the black powder magazine. It is a possibility that one of the modified 16-inch A.P. projectiles, which the Japanese used for bombs might have penetrated the 4¼-inch STS armored deck and initiated a fire followed by a detonation of the smokeless powder magazines. This seems rather improbable though, considering the small charge of explosive (less than 70 pounds of TNT) in this type of bomb, and the fact (pictures 46-208) that the initial fire was definitely above the waterline and of large-scale proportions. On the other hand, the detonation of 1000 pounds of black powder could easily initiate a detonation of the 14-inch smokeless powder. The black powder could have detonated either as the result of a bomb detonation below the third deck or a fire above the third deck passing down to the black powder magazines thru open hatches in the armored deck. From the evidence, it is believed that the latter is more probable. In any event, the six 14-inch and the two 5-inch smokeless powder magazines detonated.

14. The collapse of the foremast structure was not due, among other curious things, to the main magazine detonation. A bomb which hit and detonated close to the port leg of the tripod at the superstructure deck level severed the port leg, and the starboard leg was insufficient to prevent forward collapse. Turret I with its barbette fell vertically approximately 22 feet, and turret II with its barbette fell approximately 23 feet. All other structure above the top edge of the side armor between frames 10 and 70 was completely demolished—in fact, most of it was missing. The armor belt remained substantially in place. There were short pieces of the shell projecting almost horizontally outward at the top of the armor belt on both sides.

The next morning what remained of Arizona *was on the bottom.* Tennessee, *damaged but afloat, is visible forward of her wreck. To the left of* Tennessee, *hidden by the toppled foremast, is* West Virginia, *which was also on the bottom.*

Arizona's *bridge and foremast toppled as the forepart of the ship caved in; then the wreck burned, blackening the light gray paint of her Measure 14 camouflage. Note pedestal for a SC radar antenna atop the forward fire control tower and the two MK 33 5-inch gun directors at upper bridge level.*

15. Summarizing, there seems to be no doubt that at least one bomb struck and penetrated the forecastle deck in the vicinity of either turret I or turret II. This bomb, and possibly others, caused an intense fire which shortly covered the entire forecastle. Oil on the surface of the water was ignited. Approximately 7 seconds after the start of the fire and after the initial bomb detonation, the main magazines exploded, almost completely destroying the ship forward of frame 70. Undoubtedly, the smokeless powder magazines detonated en masse. Whether this mass detonation resulted from a bomb detonation within either the smokeless powder or black powder magazines or whether it was initiated by fire traveling down thru open hatches to the black powder magazine is unknown; but the time involved between the first bomb detonation and the detonation of the main magazines (approximately 7 seconds) and the visible intense fire above the waterline makes the latter supposition the more reasonable.

Had the primary bomb hit been down the funnel, it is unlikely that *Arizona* would have suffered nearly as bad as she did. The fires resulting from the magazine explosion took two days to extinguish and 1104 of her crew perished. Many accounts of the loss claim that *Arizona* also sustained torpedo hits, but she was protected by the USS *Vestal* moored outboard to her and the Navy divers were unable to find evidence of torpedo damage. Surveyed and found unsalvageable, *Arizona* was removed from the Navy List on 1 December 1942.

Two of Arizona's *5-inch/51 guns salvaged from her wreck; in the background is the destroyer* Cassin *under salvage.*

Hawaii Operation

The attack on Hawaii, was referred to by the Japanese as the "Hawaii Operation." It had been planned down to the last detail over a period of many months. Late in 1940 Rear Admiral Shigeru Fukudome and Admiral Isoroku Yamamoto talked over the idea. Yamamoto wanted a naval aviator to develop a surprise air attack, and the job was turned over to Rear Admiral Takajiro Ohnishi. At an Imperial Conference on 6 September 1941 the decision was made to put the plan into operation.

Because of the narrow channels in Pearl Harbor, the Japanese had to modify the controls of their torpedoes so as to need only a very short and shallow run in order to arm themselves. They also converted armor-peircing projectiles intended for use in battleship guns to use as aerial bombs (as previously mentioned).

They assembled all the ships for the attack group at a remote harbor in the Kurile Islands. Ships arrived there over a period of several days, so as to avoid any signs of a mass fleet movement. The ships were to swing far across the North Pacific, out of the usual steamer lanes, and then slant southward to Hawaii. First the Japanese sent a steamer, the *Taiyo Maru*, over the intended route, to make certain that it was safe for their purpose.

The Japanese knew that the U. S. Navy sent patrol planes out as far as 600 miles from Hawaii, so they had to run in to the launching point at night to avoid air search. As their planes had a limited range at high speed, they had to launch from a point close-in to the islands. Launch time was set at sunrise, so the planes could reach their targets just at 8 a.m.

The complete plan ran to 150 pages. Seven hundred copies were prepared and issued to the officers involved, on 5 November 1941. The Japanese fleet assigned to the operation included six aircraft carriers, two battleships, three cruisers, nine destroyers, seven tankers, and twenty-eight submarines. Five of the submarines carried midget two-man subs "piggyback" fashion. Although none of the Japanese ships were sighted before, during, or after the raid, every one of them was sunk before the war ended.

The Japanese launched their first wave of 183 aircraft in a fifteen minute period beginning at 6 a.m. when the carriers were about 230 miles north of Hawaii. The planes were over targets at Pearl Harbor, and elsewhere on Oahu, from 7:55 to 8:25 a.m. The second attack wave of 181 aircraft arrived over Pearl Harbor at about 8:40 and left around 9:45. The Japanese reported twenty-nine of their aircraft were lost.

For a time it appeared that Arizona *might be salvaged; her remaining above-water superstructure was cut away to lighten the wreck.*

The Pearl Harbor Attack

The first warning any American had of the disaster about to strike Pearl Harbor was the sudden appearance of planes flying low and fast over Merry Point, heading toward Ford Island and Battleship Row. Because men were on deck on every ship in the harbor, standing by to make morning colors at 8 a.m., or preparing to get the first liberty boat to the beach, the planes were seen almost simultaneously by hundreds of people, and because the planes had pre-selected target areas, the war actually started all over the place, all at once. It is impossible for any one account to cover what happened at Pearl Harbor in the short time the raid went on, or even to describe everything that happened aboard the *Arizona* in the very few minutes between the first bomb explosion and the time she settled to the bottom, a blazing wreck.

As the planes flashed in over the harbor, men throughout the *Arizona* were finishing breakfast, getting ready to go ashore, or preparing to go on watch. Down in the wardroom pantry, Henry Cruz, one of the stewards (and the only Guamanian, to get off the ship) was having his third cup of coffee for the morning. He and another steward had been Christmas shopping in Honolulu on Saturday, and didn't get back to the ship until 2 o'clock in the morning. Cruz heard some dull bumps, and

Lieutenant Commander Fuqua came running out of the wardroom saying, "What's going on here? Let's check topside."

Topside was a shambles by the time they reached the quarterdeck: fire, smoke, dead and dying men, and others so shocked by the devastation they just stood looking at it and crying. Cruz watched men jumping overboard into water covered with burning oil—some were already burned before they jumped, and never came up. He finally got off the ship, but his friend, who had been steward to Rear Admiral Isaac Kidd, never made it.

The skipper, Captain Franklin Van Valkenburgh, had reached the bridge, as had the division commander, Rear Admiral Isaac Kidd; a few men saw the admiral helping with a machine gun, but after the ship blew up they were not seen again.

Only a few men escaped from the forward part of the ship. The crew of the port AA director were among them. When the ship blew up, they were completely surrounded by smoke and fire and one man in the crew just vanished. Finally Seaman Russell Lott, wrapped in a blanket for protection from the heat, managed to get the attention of someone on *Vestal*, alongside. A heaving line was sent over, the director crew hauled in another line on the end of it and secured it to the director platform. Then, like a band of monkeys, they went hand over hand along the line to the *Vestal*.

The men assigned to battle stations at machine gun and searchlight platforms on the mainmast were in a good spot to see the battle, but they were unable to take any part in it, as power went out before they could fire a shot. Seaman Vernon Travioli had been standing on the starboard blister top when the first bomb struck, and he saw a plane wearing the big red Japanese "meatball" pass right over the ship. By the time he and seaman Coplin reached the searchlight platform aft, a hundred feet above the water, phones had been knocked out.

A good many other *Arizona* survivors reached Ford island during the raid—many of them burned or injured, and without much in the way of clothing.

Another man to make it off the mainmast was Marine Private R. J. McCurdy. He had just been relieved as Admiral Kidd's orderly and was in the head, getting "spit-shined" for liberty, when the ship was first hit. He reached the searchlight platform in time to see the bomb hit just aft of turret No. 4. En route, he found Second Lieutenant Simonson, dead from shrapnel. He saw the ship open up forward, like a flower, when the magazines went. There was no point in staying where they were, so McCurdy and a few others climbed down the tripod leg to the main deck. Men were crawling out of the fire forward, burned, black, and wounded. Some of them jumped over the side into the burning water and McCurdy heard them sizzle. His group, too, went overboard and headed for Ford Island, with Major Shapley leading them through the water like a mother duck with her brood. Corporal Earl Nightengale was unable to swim so Shapley carried him piggyback.

45

In the "bird bath" on the mainmast, Harvey Milhorn, a third class gunners mate, manned the machine guns with Russell Tanner. Milhorn had time to send an ammunition working party of seven seamen down to the magazines—but they were all killed when the magazines went. Milhorn was another one who made the swim to Ford Island, but Tanner was killed before he left the ship. Not everyone had to swim; the barge assigned to Admiral Kidd came alongside to help in rescue work. One of the mainmast machine gun crews, Vernon Olsen, James Vessels, and Richard Probst got to ride the admiral's barge—something mere seamen didn't do very often.

Other boats went into the rescue business with unofficial crews. John D. Anderson swam out to an abandoned motor launch in the channel and brought it alongside. Charles Otterman got out of turret No. 4, swam to Ford Island, got himself a motor launch in the confusion and brought it back under the starboard boat crane to load survivors. One motor launch went along Battleship Row picking up survivors but on the second trip to Hospital Point it was hit and went to pieces.

Men in the after 14-inch turrets were soon driven out by smoke from fires set by the bomb that struck near turret No. 4. Lieutenant Commander Fuqua, the senior surviving officer on board, went aft to help fight fire there, but by that time there was no power and no pressure on the firemains. Men used a few CO_2 fire extinguishers; which were no more effective than spitting on the fire. Fuqua (who won the Medal of Honor for his work that morning) then set about loading wounded men into anything that floated, to get them to Ford Island. About 9 a.m. he sent Ensigns Lenning and Miller below, to search for the admiral and the captain. By that time water was knee-deep in the wardroom area, and neither officer could be found.

Seaman first class Lloyd Coole, whose job it was to keep the starboard quarterdeck clean where Admiral Kidd liked to walk, was assigned to a handling room in turret No. 3. By the time he got his phones on, the ship went dark and gas fumes and smoke began pouring out of the blowers. Men climbed out of the turrets and handling rooms, but things looked so bad on deck that a few of them returned to the comparative safety of the turrets. Finally, they all headed for Ford Island. On the way, Coole was passed by third class Gunners Mate Burke, who even with his shoes on made much better time. Others from No. 3 turret who made the island were John Doucett and Richard Hauff, (although Hauff still doesn't remember how he did it) and Carl Christiansen, Jr., an 18-year old recruit seaman who had been on the ship for less than a month.

About the only survivors from battle stations in the forward part of the ship were men who never got to them. One of these was Russell Warriner, a seaman whose station was in sky control, on the foremast. He was still eating breakfast when someone ran through the compartment yelling "The Japs are here!" Warriner headed for his battle station but got no farther than the boat deck when something hit him on the back of the head. The next thing he remembered was the sight of dead and wounded men, a whaleboat in the water blowing up, and the sheer horror of the *Oklahoma* capsizing like a huge harpooned whale, and the cries of men who scrambled along her sides as she went over. Then the forward magazines went; somehow he found his way to the quarterdeck and two men put him in a boat for Ford Island.

Seaman William Parker got to his battle station, at No. 1 5-inch AA gun, along with two other men. They fired the gun until the ship blew up and Parker was blown overboard. The next thing Parker remembered was lying in the water at the edge of Ford Island. His shoes and all of his clothing had been blown off in the explosion. For his courage in keeping the gun firing as long as he could, he was later awarded the Navy Cross. Seaman Clay Musick's battle station was in the port AA magazine, but he didn't get there. He was shining brightwork in a motorboat when the first bomb hit; the second one knocked him down, breaking his hip, and a passing tug hauled him aboard.

Louis Pacetti was another survivor from the area of the foremast. Although most *Arizona* survivors were soon at sea with the fleet, Pacetti was one of the men retained at Pearl Harbor to help with salvage work on the sunken ships. As a diver, he spent more than a hundred hours crawling around through the dark dangerous wrecks. One day in 1943 he worked his way below deck on the *Arizona*, found his locker, and opened it to recover his fountain pen and rosary.

Casualties at Pearl Harbor

The U. S. Navy and the U. S. Marine Corps had 2,117 officers and men killed or fatally wounded, 779 wounded men survived. The Army had 218 officers and men killed or fatally wounded; 364 others were wounded, and 22 were missing. The Navy lost 98 aircraft and had 31 damaged; the Army lost 64 aircraft.

The battleships *Oklahoma*, *Arizona*, and target ship *Utah* were sunk. The battleships *California* and *West Virginia*, and minelayer *Oglala* were sunk, but were raised and returned to service. The battleships *Nevada*, *Pennsylvania*, *Tennessee*, and *Maryland*, cruisers *Raleigh*, *Honolulu*, and *Helena*, destroyers *Cassin*, *Shaw*, and *Downes*, and auxiliary ships *Curtiss* and *Vestal* were damaged, but repaired.

Only Battery Pennsylvania was completed, and it was test-fired on VJ-Day when it instantly became obsolete.

Only the after turrets were salvaged from the Arizona. *They were to be installed in two Coast Artillery sites designated Battery Pennsylvania and Battery Arizona on the island of Oahu. Here armor is being assembled for Battery Pennsylvania, 22 March 1945.*

Arizona's *After Turrets*

When the Navy determined the *Arizona* to be unsalvageable because of the almost total destruction of the center section of her hull, the Army immediately became interested in the possibility of incorporating her 14-inch guns into the coast defense system of Oahu.

The after section of *Arizona* remained almost intact after the sinking of the ship and in early 1942 it was discovered that the two after turrets were not as seriously damaged as they were originally thought to be. Planning began in June 1942 and approval to proceed was given in October; the two turrets, designated as Batteries Pennsylvania and Arizona, were to be placed on the tip of Mokapu Peninsula, to cover the eastern approaches of Oahu, and near Kahe Point, to cover the south and west, respectively.

The design of the installations required some seven months: each consisting of an extensive underground system of tunnels and galleries converging on a massive concrete barbette atop which was mounted one of *Arizona*'s turrets at ground level. Each battery was self-contained, generating its own power and provisioned for local defense in the event of a possible siege.

Construction of the installations began in April 1943 and proceeded very slowly. The immense undertaking was plagued with many problems, which, in many cases were not easily overcome. The removal of the turrets from the wreck was begun before the planning of the shore batteries had been completed and much vital structure had been cut away. Transportation of the turret parts and guns to their new sites became a complex operation. Major turret segments were barged to the beaches below the battery sites where special roads were constructed up to the barbettes. The new batteries were somewhat larger internally than their shipboard counterparts, requiring the manufacture of additional ammunition hoists and other equipment. Many damaged parts and components had to be repaired and remanufactured. Engineering drawings and technical information were not always available, and in some cases where they were, the components had to be redesigned to fit the new installation.

Battery Pennsylvania was finally completed in August 1945, and was first test fired on VJ-Day which announced Japan's surrender on Oahu. Battery Arizona, still incomplete at the end of the war, was suspended and construction was never resumed. A few years later, when the United States decided to discontinue fixed coastal defenses, Batteries Arizona and Pennsylvania were cut up for scrap along with other American seacoast weapons and fortifications. All that now remains of the batteries are concrete lined holes of impressive size.

The Arizona Memorial

For years after the Pearl Harbor attack, the burned-out hulk of the *Arizona* was a vivid reminder of that day, and ships of the fleet began the unofficial practice of rendering honors—saluting the wreck—as other ships had done when she was in commission. On 7 March 1950 Admiral Arthur W. Radford, Commander in Chief of the Pacific Fleet, issued an official order: "From today on the USS *Arizona* will again fly our country's flag . . ." Several years later the Commandant of the Fourteenth Naval District invited the Pacific War Memorial Commission to sponsor a program to obtain a suitable memorial for the ship, and as a result, on 15 March 1958 the 85th Congress authorized the construction of such a memorial.

The result is undoubtedly one of the most impressive structures ever erected as a memorial. Designed by Alfred Preis, it is in the form of an enclosed bridge, 184 feet long, 36 feet wide, and 21 feet high at the ends, which tapers to 27 feet wide and 14 feet high at the center. It sits on pilings driven into the harbor bottom; no part of it touches the hulk of the *Arizona* which can be seen just below the surface of the water. The most notable feature of the memorial is the shrine room, where a wall of Italian marble is inscribed with the names of the men who died when the ship was destroyed. The oldest relic in the memorial is the bell that the *Arizona* mounted when she was commissioned on 17 October 1916.

Since the formal dedication of the memorial—where the U. S. flag flies every day—millions of people from the United States and Japan have visited there, arriving for various reasons and departing with various emotions. The visitors for whom the memorial has the deepest meaning still proudly call themselves *Arizona* sailors; they are the men who were there on 7 December 1941 and who return to read the names of other *Arizona* sailors who are still there. For all the men in the *Arizona* on 7 December 1941, the memorial assures that the date

> *. . . shall ne'er go by*
> *From this day to the ending of the world,*
> *But we in it shall be remembered,—*
> *We few, we happy few, we band of brothers; . . .*
> —King Henry V, Act IV.

Nearly twenty years after Arizona's *loss, the carrier* Bennington *renders honors, as do all U.S. Naval vessels, as she passes her wreck. This aerial photograph shows most of the hull just below the surface and still leaking oil. The remains of turret No. 2, and two 1.1 inch gun tubs are clearly visible abreast the flag pole.*

Regular color ceremonies have been held aboard the wreck of Arizona *since 1 March 1950. This daily practice was established by Admiral A. W. Radford and the original ceremony is shown in the photograph at left.*

On 15 March 1958 the Congress authorized a permanent memorial to be built over the wreck of Arizona. Completed on 30 May 1962, it serves as a lasting reminder of the 1,177 men entombed there.

DEDICATED
TO THE ETERNAL MEMORY
OF OUR GALLANT SHIPMATES
IN THE USS ARIZONA
WHO GAVE THEIR LIVES IN ACTION
7 DECEMBER 1941

"FROM TODAY ON THE USS ARIZONA
WILL AGAIN FLY OUR COUNTRY'S FLAG
JUST AS PROUDLY AS SHE DID ON THE
MORNING OF 7 DECEMBER 1941.
I AM SURE THE ARIZONA'S CREW WILL
KNOW AND APPRECIATE WHAT WE ARE
DOING" ADMIRAL A.W. RADFORD, USN
7 MARCH 1950

MAY GOD MAKE HIS FACE
TO SHINE UPON THEM
AND GRANT THEM PEACE

Left, the plaque dedicated by Admiral A. W. Radford beginning the daily color ceremonies aboard Arizona's wreck.

The outline of Arizona's hull is clearly visible in the photograph at right. Note that the bow remains intact and the structure between it and turret No. 2 has been destroyed.

GENERAL DATA-1916

Name | ARIZONA
Hull Number | BB-39
Builder | New York Navy Yard, Brooklyn, New York
Laid Down | 16 March 1914
Launched | 19 June 1915
Commissioned | 17 October 1917

Displacement:

31,400 tons Standard
32,567 tons Full Load

Dimensions:
608' 0'' Length Overall
600' 0'' Waterline Length
97'' 0½'' Maximum Beam
28' 10'' Mean Draft
29' 10'' Max. Draft at Full Load
Construction Cost:
$7,425,000 (hull and machinery)
$12,993,579.23 (total)

ARMOR PROTECTION (*See* Armor Diagram

Total Armor Weight: 8,072 tons.
Belt: Frame 20 to 127: 13.5'' from top of second deck to 2'4'' below normal waterline, then taper uniformly to 8'' to bottom 8'9¾'' below waterline=17'4 5/8'' Total Height.
Frame 127 to sternpost: 13'' from top of third deck to 2'4'' below normal waterline, then taper as above.
Ends: Forward at Frame 20: 13'' between second deck and second platform, tapering to 8'' below first platform (total depth 17' 4 5/8'')
Aft at Frame 127: 13'' between second and third decks.
Aftermost: Athwartship from just abaft rudder stock to third deck: 13'' down to 2'4'' below normal waterline, tapering uniformly to 8'' at bottom 8'9¾'' below waterline.
Decks: 120-lb. protective deck covering armor belt. Splinter deck; 40-lb. on flat and 60-lb. on slope behind belt. (40.8 lb. = 1'')

Uptakes: Octagonal tapering shield surrounding stack uptakes between second and upper decks: 15'' sides; 12'' quarter plates; 9'' ends.
Turrets: Face plates: 18''; Sides: 9'' increased to 10'' near front; Rear: 9''; Top: 5''; exposed undersides: 2''.
Barbettes: 13'' above second deck; 4½'' between second and third decks.
Conning Tower: 16'' sides; two 4'' layers on top.
Conning Tower tube: 5-ft. inside diameter from 3rd deck to Conning Tower base; 16'' armor above 2nd deck, 6'' below.
Longitudinal Torpedo Bulkheads: Two Continuous each side from Frame 20 to 127; 60-lb. STS plating outer bulkhead, normal structural steel inner bulkhead. Total width of protection each side: 11'9''.
Transverse Torpedo Bulkheads: Four 40-lb. STS bulkheads outboard the outer longitudinal bulkhead at Frames 23, 30, 90, and 120.

MACHINERY

Total Weight: 2,462 tons (with liquids).
Boilers: TWELVE Babcock & Wilcox; 55,332 sq. ft. total heating surface.
Turbines: EIGHT Parsons-type turbines on four shafts: Two High Pressure ahead (one right-hand, one left) and two High Pressure astern (one right-handed, one left) on inboard shafts; two Low Pressure ahead and astern (one right-handed, one left) and two cruising turbines on outboard shafts. All shafts turn outboard ahead.
Shaft Horsepower: 34,000 max. ahead.
Maximum Speed: 21.0 knots at 226 shaft RPM.
Endurance: 19 knots = 3,240 naut. miles. 15 knots = 4,750 naut. miles (on cruising turbines).
15 knots = 4,570 naut. miles (on main turbines).

10 knots = 6,950 naut. miles (on cruising turbines).
(*assumes 95% futel consumable*)
Generators: FOUR 300kw, 240-volt DC turbo-generator sets.
Propellers: FOUR 4-bladed, 12'01½'' diameter.
Rudders: ONE, balanced, tapered type; 443-sq. ft. area. Train limits 38'' to port and starboard.
Fuel Oil: 2,332 tons (694,830 gallons).
Reserve Boiler Feed Water: 313.5 tons.
Potable Water: 187.5 tons.
Anchors: THREE 20,000-lb. each (two to port one starboard); 180 fathoms chain to port anchors, 120 fathoms to starboard.
COMPLEMENT: 1,087 total (56 officers; 1.031 enlisted, including 72 Marines).

GENERAL DATA-1941

Reconstructed: Norfolk Navy Yard, July 1929 to Feb. 1931.

Recommissioned: 1 March 1931.

Modernization Cost: $5,290,000.00

Sunk: 7 December 1941 (Stricken from Naval Register 1 Dec. 1942).

Memorial Authorized: 16 May 1958 (SECNAV Notice 5340).

PROTECTION

Armor: As before, except for addition of a supplementary layer of 70-lb. STS horizontal plating (approx. 1.7'') for bomb protection on the second deck and an armored grating within the funnel at the upper deck level.

MACHINERY

Boilers: SIX Bureau Express-type; 300-psi/472°F. operating Temperature.
Turbines: FOUR Westinghouse geared Impulse/Reaction 3,600 RPM High Pressure Main Turbines; Four Westinghouse geared Impulse/Reaction 3,600 RPM cruise turbines; Four Parsons 226 RPM Low Pressure ahead and astern turbines; Four Parsons 226 RPM High Pressure astern turbines.
Shaft Horsepower: 35,081 max. ahead (10-hr. trial, July 1931).
Maximum Speed: 20.7 knots (trial July 1931).
Endurance: 20 knots = 8,500 naut. miles. 15 knots = 13,600 naut. miles.
Generators: FOUR 300kw 120/240-volt DC turbo-generator sets.

Displacement:
37,654 tons Full Load (trial 1931).
34,207 tons Normal.
32,600 tons Standard (Washington Treaty Measurement).
Dimensions:
608'0'' Length Overall
600'0'' Waterline Length
106'2¾'' Maximum Beam
28'10'' Mean Draft
30'1¾'' Full Load Draft
33'3'' Emergency Load Draft

Longitudinal Torpedo Protection: Width increased to 19 ft. each side by the addition of 4'7 1/8'' bulges to each side between Frames 17 and 134 and the provision of two additional longitudinal internal bulkheads between Frames 20 and 127.

Propellers: FOUR three-bladed, 12'7'' diameter.
Rudder: as in 1916.
Fuel Oil: 4,630 tons normal/6,180 tons emergency.
Diesel Oil: 75 tons (for boats).
Gasoline: 11.76 tons (for aircraft).
Lubricating Oil: 5,000 gallons.
Reserve Boiler Feed Water: 323 tons normal plus 392 tons additional emergency capacity.
Potable Water: 402 tons.
Complement: 1,731 total (92 officers and warrants; 1,639 enlisted).
Accommodations: 2,037 Total (4 Cabin Officers; 44 Wardroom Officers; 32 Junior Officers; 10 Warrant Officers; 72 Chief Petty Officers; 1,875 other enlisted).

Acknowledgements - we are grateful to Dr. Dean C. Allard and his staff of the Navy Department, Operational Archives Branch for their assistance with General Board material; and the Old Military Records Section of the National Archives. Dr. Tom Hone provided essential material on the loss of Arizona, and Dr. E. R. Lewis provided an account of the use of her turrets in Hawaii.

ARMAMENT SUMMARY

Guns/TT	Mounting	Oct. 1916	May 1917	Aug 1918	June 1922	March 1931	Dec. 1941	Proposed
14''/45 Mk. 3	Triple	12	12	12	12	12	12	12
5''/51 Mk. 15	Single Mk. 13	22	22	14	14	12	10	—
5''/38 Mk. 12	Twin Mk. 32	—	—	—	—	—	—	16
5''/25 Mk. 11	Single Mk. 19	—	—	—	—	8	8	—
3''/50 Mk. 21	Single Mk. 13	—	4	4	8	—	—	—
40mm/60 Mk.1/2	Quad Mk. 2	—	—	—	—	—	—	16
1.1''/75 Mk. 1	Quad Mk. 2	—	—	—	—	—	—	16
20mm/70 Mk. 4	Single Mk. 4	—	—	—	—	—	—	16
.50/63.8	Single	—	—	—	—	8	8	—
21'' Mk. 3 TT	Single, submerged	2	2	2	2	—	—	—

Note: In addition to the above, in 1941 *Arizona* carried two 3-pounder saluting cannon on the bridge deck and four one-pounder sub-caliber guns, one atop each 14'' turret for firing practice. She also carried practice loading machines for the 5''/51 caliber guns and the 5''/25 AA guns. On completion, she carried four 3-pounder saluting cannon, one 3'' landing gun for the boats, two 1-pounder boat guns, and two .30 caliber machine guns.

BALLISTIC DATA

Gun	Type	Model MK	Weight lb.	L Cal.	Explosive Charge lb.	Explosive Charge %	Firing§ Charge	Muzzle Velocity fps	el.	Surface Range yards	AA el.	AA Range alt.(ft.)	AP-MK Armor V & H	PB	16,900	19,000	21,000	23,000
14''/45 MK 1 SP M 1911, World War I RPM: 1.5*	APCBC	(1918)	1400	3.5	31.5	2.25	365	2600	15°	21.000			Angle of fall° SV - (fps) Mk V'' Mk H''	0° 23.1'' —	15° 13.2'' 3.7''		22.5° 10.9'' 4.2''	
14''/45 MK 1 SP M 1911, 1930 RPM: 1.5*	APCBC	(1930)	1400	3.7	31.5	2.25	420	2700	15°	24,000			Angle of fall° SV - (fps) Mk V'' Mk H''	0° 25.3'' —	15° 14.3'' 3.9''		22.5° 11.8'' 4.5''	
14''/45 MK 8 SP M 1911, World War II RPM: 1.5*	APCBC HC	20 19	1500 1275	† †	22.9 104.2	1.5 8.2	420 420	2600 2735	15° 15°	23,000 23,500			Angle of fall° SV - (fps) Mk V'' Mk H''	0° 26.4'' —		15° 15.2'' 4.2''		22.5° 12.9'' 4.9''

														PB	9,000	11,800‡	12,000	17,100‡
5''/51 MK 13 SP M 1909 RPM: 8-10	Com. Com. HC	(1918) 15 39	50 50 50	3.5 4.5 4.5	2.04 2.14 13.2	4.1 4.3 26.4	24.5 24.5 24.5	3150 3150 3150	15° 20° 20°	12,000 17,100 17,100			Angle of fall° SV - (fps) Mk V'' Mk H''	0° 3150 6.4'' —	15° 895 1.4'' 0.4''	15° 2.1'' 0.6''	22.5° 800 1.25'' 0.5''	22.5° 1.1'' 0.6''

														PB	7,000	10,400	14,600	
3''/50 MK 21 DP RPM: 12-15	APCBC HC AAC	29 27 27	13.1 13.1 13.1	4.1 4.1 4.1	0.16 0.74 0.74	1.2 5.7 5.7	4.0 4.0 4.0	2700 2700 2700	45°	14,600	85°	29,800	Angle of fall° SV - (fps) Mk V'' Mk H''	0° 2700 6.0'' 0	15° 1.5'' 0.4''	30° 0.75'' 0.4''	57.5° 0.375'' 0.8''	
40 mm (1.57''/60)** MK 1-2 40 mm M 1942 RPM: 160	AP AAC	81 1-2	2.0 2.0				315 gr.	2890 2890	42° 42°	11,000 11,000	90°	22,800	Angle of fall° SV - (fps) Mk V'' Mk H''					
1.10''/75 MK 1 28 mm M 1939 RPM: 150	AAC	1-2	0.92				120 gr.	2700	41°	7,400	90°	19,000	Angle of fall° SV - (fps) Mk V'' Mk H''					
20 mm (0.8''/70)*** MK 4 20 mm RPM: 450	APT HE HET	9 3 7	0.269 0.271 0.271		— 0.024 0.001	— 0.9	27.7	2740	35°	4,800	90°	10,000	Angle of fall° SV - (fps) Mk V'' Mk H''					

* Fixed Loading Angle.

† With shortened windshield to fit hoists.

** AP penetrates 1.7'' @ 1,000 yards. Ranges are absolute max. Tracer burns out at 5,000 yds., hor., 15,000 ft. vert.

*** Tracer burns out at 3,000 yds.

§ Standard Charge Determination-4 sections.

‡ Comm. MK15 projectile.

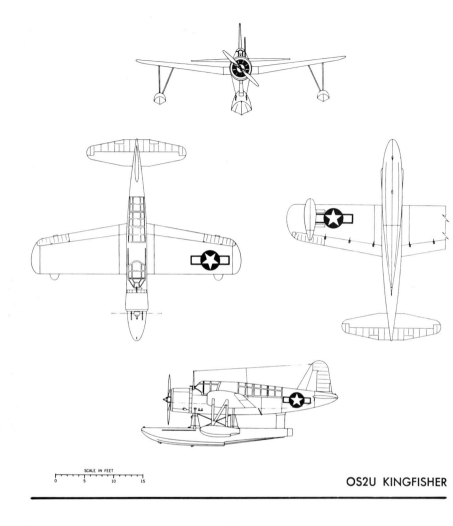

OS2U KINGFISHER

SCALE IN FEET
0　5　10　15

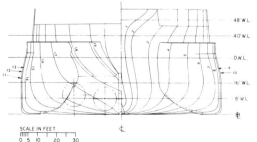

SCALE IN FEET
0 5 10   20   30

BODY PLAN

HULL NUMBER INDEX

LIST OF ABBREVIATIONS

AA—ANTIAIRCRAFT	HET—HIGH EXPLOSIVE TRACER
AAC—ANTIAIRCRAFT COMMON	H.P.—HORSEPOWER
Alt.—ALTITUDE	I.H.P.—INDICATED HORSEPOWER
AP—ARMOR PIERCING	K.C.—KRUPP CEMENTED ARMOR
APCBC—ARMOR PIERCING CAPPED/ BALLISTIC CAP	kw—KILOWATTS
	MK—MODEL DESIGNATION/NUMBER
Cal.—CALIBERS (dia. of bore)	M—MODEL YEAR
CPO—CHIEF PETTY OFFICER	L.P.—LOW PRESSURE
Com.—COMMON	PB—POINT BLANK
DP—DUAL PURPOSE	psi—POUNDS/SQ. INCH
el°—ELEVATION/DEGREES	PT—PATROL TORPEDO BOAT
Fwd.—FORWARD	RPM—ROUNDS/MIN. (ballistic)
fps—FEET/SECOND	SC—AIR SEARCH RADAR
gr.—GRAINS	SP—SINGLE PURPOSE
H—HORIZONTAL	STS—SPECIL TREATED STEEL
HC—HIGH CAPACITY	SV—STRIKING VELOCITY
HE—HIGH EXPLOSIVE	V—VERTICAL

Photograph of Arizona, *made as she was passing under the San Francisco - Oakland Bay Bridge. The SOC aircraft date this photograph, but she does not yet have the MK 33 directors or the "birdbath" of her final configuration.*